The Tower to Bispham

The Blackpool Tramway since 1960

Volume Two

Above Heading for Bispham - though from Talbot Square (North Pier) not the Tower - an English Electric railcoach leaves St Stephen's Avenue tram stop on a bitterly cold New Year's Day, 1962.

The Tower to Bispham
703

The Blackpool Tramway since 1960

Volume Two

Contents

First published 2015

Published by Rails Publishing
www.capitaltransport.com

Printed by Parksons Graphics

Left Balloon 703 approaches Lowther Avenue on 15 June 2006.

Foreword

This is the second leg of a photographic ride along the Blackpool tramway from Starr Gate to Fleetwood. Volume One - *Starr Gate to the Tower* - covered the first three miles, and Volume Two has turned out to be no quicker. As happens on the tramway, things should speed up north of Bispham.

The idea behind the journey is to show how the coastal tramway has evolved since 1960 (when I started photographing the trams), though *evolved* scarcely conveys the reality of that period. *Clinging on* might be more appropriate; clinging on - as the first and last of Britain's 200 electric tramways - in the hope of some unspecified revivalist miracle.

Against all odds, the miracle materialised in February 2008, when the Labour Government approved an £85 million scheme to rebuild and re-equip the entire tramway. The project was completed in 2012 with the opening of the Supertram system.

As with Volume One, the focus is on the tramway going about its everyday business, rather than on the tramcars themselves. For those requiring more details of the vehicles, Volume One contains an all-time fleet list, and fuller details of all the cars can be found in my book *North Pier by Tram*.

Once again I have relied on others to fill gaps in my own coverage. My thanks for information and photographs to Andrew Blood, Peter Fitton, Martin Jenkins, Malcolm King, Peter Makinson, Colin McLeod, James Millington, Dave Monaghan, Alan Robson, Clyde L. Shoebridge, Alan Spencer, Robert Townley, Paul Turner, Peter Waller, Tony Wilson and the Fylde Tramway Society.

So here are another three miles and fifty-odd years of the Blackpool tramway. I hope this book conveys some of the pleasure I've had in watching and recording what has been a remarkable half century.

Brian Turner
Lytham
April 2015

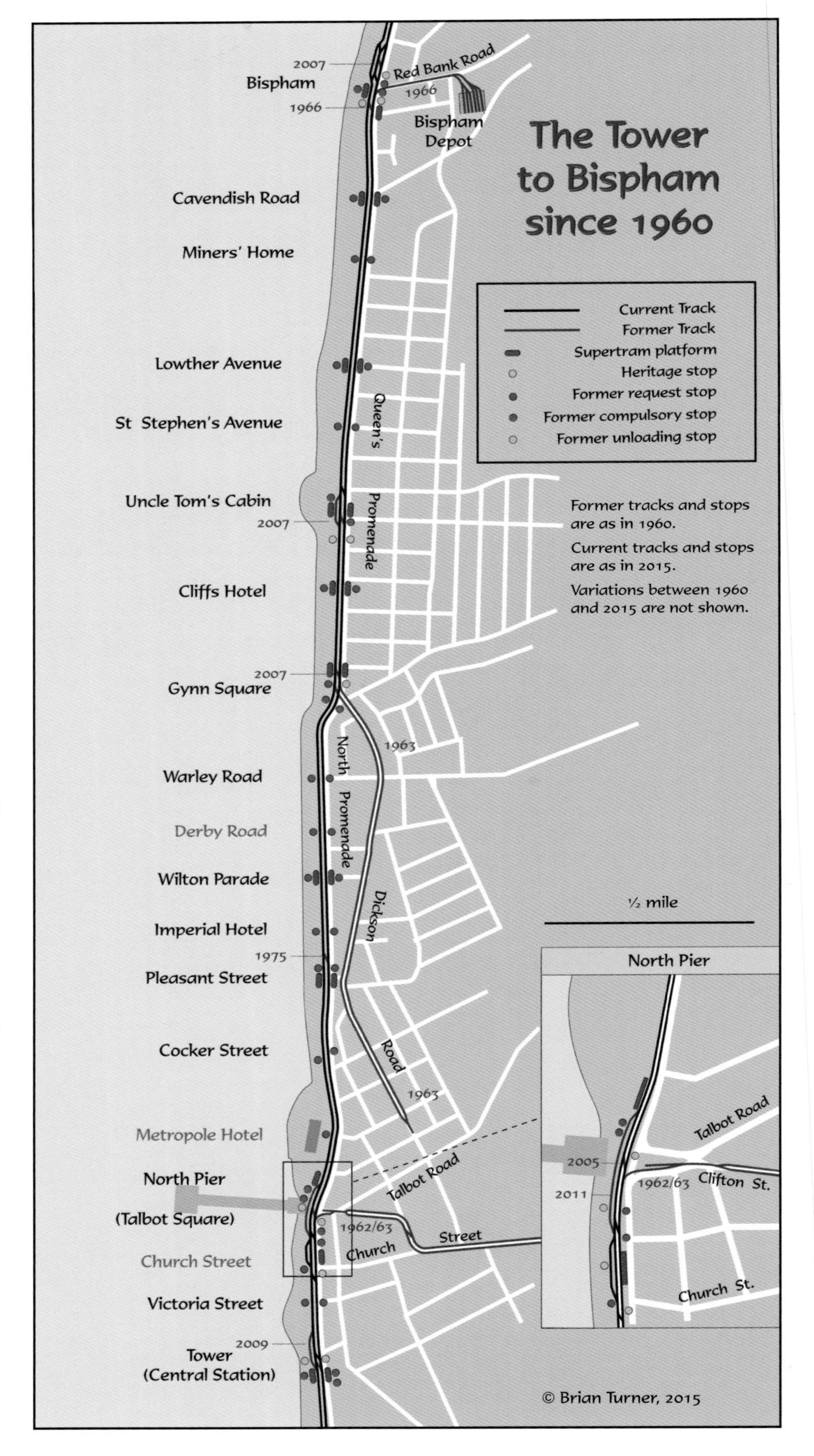

1. The Tower

Volume Two starts where Volume One left off - with King Kong ensconced above the Tower building in 1984. This chapter looks at the Tower's tramway layout in general, while Chapter Two covers the individual tram stops in detail. Here Balloon 702 heads south on 12 August.

The Tower 1961

Above The principal tramway feature at the Tower was the third track laid in June 1923, originally for the Lytham St Annes cars. On the centre of the three tracks, Standard car 40 reverses for a trip to Starr Gate in August 1961. No. 40's guard has to wait for Coronation 317, running late and turning short at the Pleasure Beach. Balloon 257, on the high-season Starr Gate - Thornton Gate service, edges up from the unloading stop, whilst in the distance a new twin-car heads north on a limited-stop run to Little Bispham. Four generations of Blackpool tram.

Below Looking south from the three-track layout on 8 July 1961, former toastrack No. 166 is returning to Rigby Road after a live broadcast for ABC Television's *Holiday Town Parade*.

Tower Bridge

In March 1975 a concrete footbridge was erected over the line, just south of the three-track layout.

Top The Tower bridge was rarely so busy, but on 12 June 1976 it was an ideal vantage point to watch a parade for the Centenary of Blackpool. Dreadnought 59 is reversing.

Centre The bridge from the south, with Centenary car 641 approaching the Tower on 29 July 1984, three weeks after entering service.

Below Although hardly a thing of beauty, the bridge offered a fine view of the three-track layout. On 15 August 1979, twin-car 675/685 waits for OMO car 6 to depart northwards. Permanent Way bus 437 (former PD/2 337) stands by the northbound shelter. In the foreground is the non-tram Adshel (*see page 24*) which was moved north when the bridge was built.

The Tower in Winter

Above On 26 January 1979, OMO car 9 adds a splash of colour after a snowfall which highlights the tramway accoutrements at the Tower - concrete fencing, the steel northbound shelter with inspector's cabin, the seasonal stop for tour cars, and two unloading stops, the southbound one - for some reason - lettered in red. The roadway remains untreated, with council workers on strike during the so-called Winter of Discontent.

Below Snowplough-fitted Balloon 723 sets off for Rigby Road on 14 December 1981, leaving the other snowplough, No. 722, to cool down after overheating.

Hold the Front Page

On 1 February 2002 the Tower bridge was the vantage point for this spectacular picture, which was spread across the front page of next day's *Daily Telegraph*. Jubilee 762 is being towed to higher ground at North Pier by tower wagon 940 after becoming stuck in debris from a 32 feet tide whipped up by a gale, while working the 12.22 from Starr Gate. (*John Giles, Press Association*)

Threesomes at the Tower

Above A happy conjunction of historic - if not strictly historical - liveries on 24 July 2006. Balloon 700 is flanked by Boat 605, wearing the same wartime livery (which no Boat genuinely did), and by sister car 604 in 1990s colour scheme - equally speculative.

Below Three reversible twin-cars at the Tower on 22 June 1984, all running trailer-south and all in the same livery, though the painters seem to have been in three minds about where to put the fleet number. 685 was painted in May 1965, 686 in November 1969, and 682 in December 1964, but none of them saw the Paint Shop again until the 1990s - possibly the longest an operational Blackpool tram ever went without a repaint.

Above Come On, England! But 715's patriotic cry was in vain. The nation's World Cup hopes had already been cruelly extinguished by Portugal in a penalty shoot-out when the Balloon met two retro-liveried sisters - Nos. 703 (1980s style) and 712 (1950s) on 17 July 2006.

Below Two trams and a bus (plus a Blackpool Transport lorry) on 31 July 2001. Balloon 709 waits for twin-car 672/682 to load, while running repairs are made to the crossover. In support is a short-lived Permanent Way Atlantean which came to Blackpool in 1994 with the Fylde undertaking. Originally No. 329 in the Hull fleet, it became Fylde 129, then Blackpool 489, and finally served as P.W. bus 263 from October 2000 to March 2002.

From Three Tracks to Two

Above 2009 was the last season for the Tower bridge (which was demolished in July) and the three-track layout. Centenary 648 stands at the unloading stop on 13 April.

Centre A sight which would soon disappear from the Tower. The guard stows away the bamboo pole after turning 602's trolley on 11 September 2009.

Bottom The Tower lost its loop line and shelter when the track from Central Pier to Church Street was rebuilt during the winter of 2009/10. Aptly the contractors were Bam Nuttall, who (as Edmund Nuttall) had relaid the street track between the Tower and Church Street as long ago as 1899. The overhead crew are adjusting the wiring for the replacement crossover on 14 January 2011.

Don't Fence Me In

But they did. The winter of 2010/11 saw major construction work on both sides of the relaid tramway - the new Promenade to the west, and reconstruction of the roadway to the east. Both projects continued well into 2011, so that when the trams restarted at Easter, the track was completely enclosed by security fencing, and cars ran non-stop between Central and North Piers.

Above Jubilee 762 passes the Tower building - itself being restored - on 11 May 2011.

Below The road reopened (on a shared-space basis) in June 2011. Centenary 648 again - now in advertising livery - on 31 August. Much else has changed since 648 was pictured opposite.

THE COMEDY CARPET

A popular feature of the new Promenade, between the Tower and Victoria Street, is the Comedy Carpet, which consists of 215 panels containing the names, jokes and catch-phrases of more than 1,000 entertainers who have appeared at Blackpool over the years - altogether 160,000 letters cut from red and black granite and embedded in a special concrete. Designed by Gordon Young, it took five years to make at a cost (grant-aided) of £2.6 million.

Above The Comedy Carpet was opened by Ken Dodd (*see page 133*) on 10 October 2011. Brush car 632 heads north in low afternoon sunshine on 30 October, just a week before the traditional tramway closed.

Below The best view of the Comedy Carpet is obtained from the Tower, here in May 2012 with Boat 600 passing a slightly trimmed Carpet. The eastern side (as shown above) was laid very close to the tramway, with the result that visitors stepped onto the track to read these panels, which were meant to have been laid the other way round to avoid this problem. In March 2012, shortly before the Supertram system opened, the offending five panels were removed. (*Dave Monaghan*)

Tower Turnbacks

With the opening of the Supertram system, the Tower lost most of its operational significance. However there was still a crossover, and when special events were held on the headland there, the tramway between the Tower and North Pier was closed, and cars reversed at those two places. The first of these occasions was a concert by Elton John in June 2012. On 25 June, Flexity 013 - having reversed on the Tower crossover - is released through the barrier to load at the southbound platform.

2. Tram Stops at the Tower

Tour Stop

Top In September 1956 the centre track at the Tower became the starting point for the new Tour of Illuminations. This was joined in 1958 by the Coastal Tour, operated by prototype twin-car 276/275, seen here in June that year. (*A.P. Tatt/On-line Transport Archive*)

Centre From Easter 1960 the new Promenade Circular also loaded at the stop. An added attraction that season was the use of cars restored for the 75th Anniversary. Fleetwood Box 40 and Rack 2 load on 30 July. The concrete fencing on both sides of the three-track layout was erected in 1960.

Below Although the Promenade Circular was anything but that - being a straight ride up to Little Bispham, down to Pleasure Beach and back - it was remarkably popular, as shown by the queue for an early evening ride in August 1961. The poster for the tour shows a twin-car, but open Boats were the staple fare - here No. 228, holding up a Bispham-bound railcoach under the protection of the resident inspector.

Opposite OMO car 1 loads at the southbound Tower shelter on 12 August 1984.

Northbound Stops

Above For many years the northbound stop - with a cast-iron shelter by David Rowell & Co. - was just south of the points leading to the third track, but in 1960 two stops (for unloading and loading) were opened on the loop itself. At Easter 1961 brand-new twin-car 279/T9 passes the cast-iron shelter - still with its stop sign, since the new stops weren't in use until the season started at Whitsuntide.

Below During 1960 and 1961 the new stops were used only in summer. Passing them on 18 February 1961 is railcoach 221 on the doomed Squire's Gate route. The tram itself seemed doomed, but turned out to be a born survivor. Withdrawn in 1963, No. 221 served as works car 5 for long enough to become OMO 5 in 1972. Withdrawn for a second time in 1993, No. 5 escaped the axe again in 2000, when it was acquired by the National Tramway Museum.

Northbound Stops

Above Early in 1962 the northbound stop moved permanently to the third track, and a steel shelter was erected. It is thought to have been a rebuild of one of the Squire's Gate shelters removed from North Pier and the Tower after the Lytham Road route closed in October 1961. Loading at the shelter in July 1965 is newly-reversible twin-car 272/T2. On the centre track (advertising the Royal Lancashire Show at the old Stanley Park airport) is No. 160, the only non-illuminated Standard car running that summer.

Centre In June 1968, Corporation ambulance No. 37 - summoned from its station in Blundell Street tram depot - takes a short cut past twin-car 675/685 and the old shelter. Nowadays road vehicles - and cyclists - often use the smoothly paved tram tracks, but it rarely happened with the standard of paving in the 1960s.

Bottom The cast-iron Rowell shelter remained in place, though not for tramway purposes. It is seen in June 1967 - well patronised - from the top deck of Balloon 248. The Rowell shelters were very similar to those built by Walter Macfarlane, but had different ornamentation on the castings.

Northbound Stops

Above In April 1968, Coronation No. 311 turns onto the loop line behind Z-car 318, which is loading at the northbound steel shelter.

Centre The steel shelter disappeared in favour of an Adshel in 1980, but the little inspector's cabin at the south end remained. In December 1981 the inspector collects the square rolling-pin from OMO 12's driver during relaying of the southbound line between Tower and North Pier.

Bottom 'Snug' would perhaps be the most charitable adjective for the cabin, seen with its resident inspector on 12 December 1981. OMO 12 again - this time northbound. The stop sign is attached to the end of the new Adshel.

Heritage Shelter

The northbound Tower stop received this heritage-style shelter in 1994. Balloon 706 loads on 2 September 2008.

Standard 147 leaves the heritage shelter at dusk on 8 September 2007.

Northbound Stops

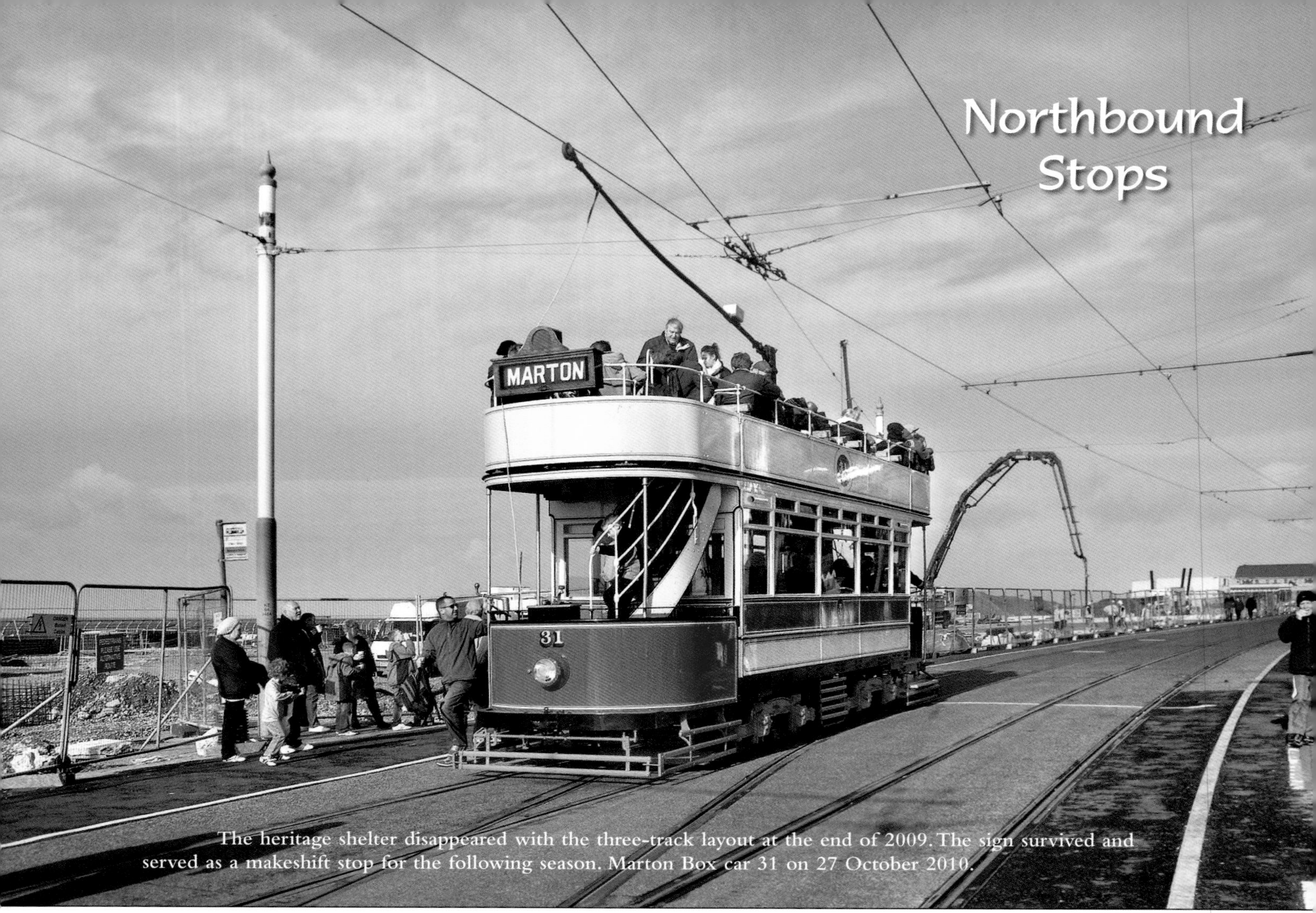

The heritage shelter disappeared with the three-track layout at the end of 2009. The sign survived and served as a makeshift stop for the following season. Marton Box car 31 on 27 October 2010.

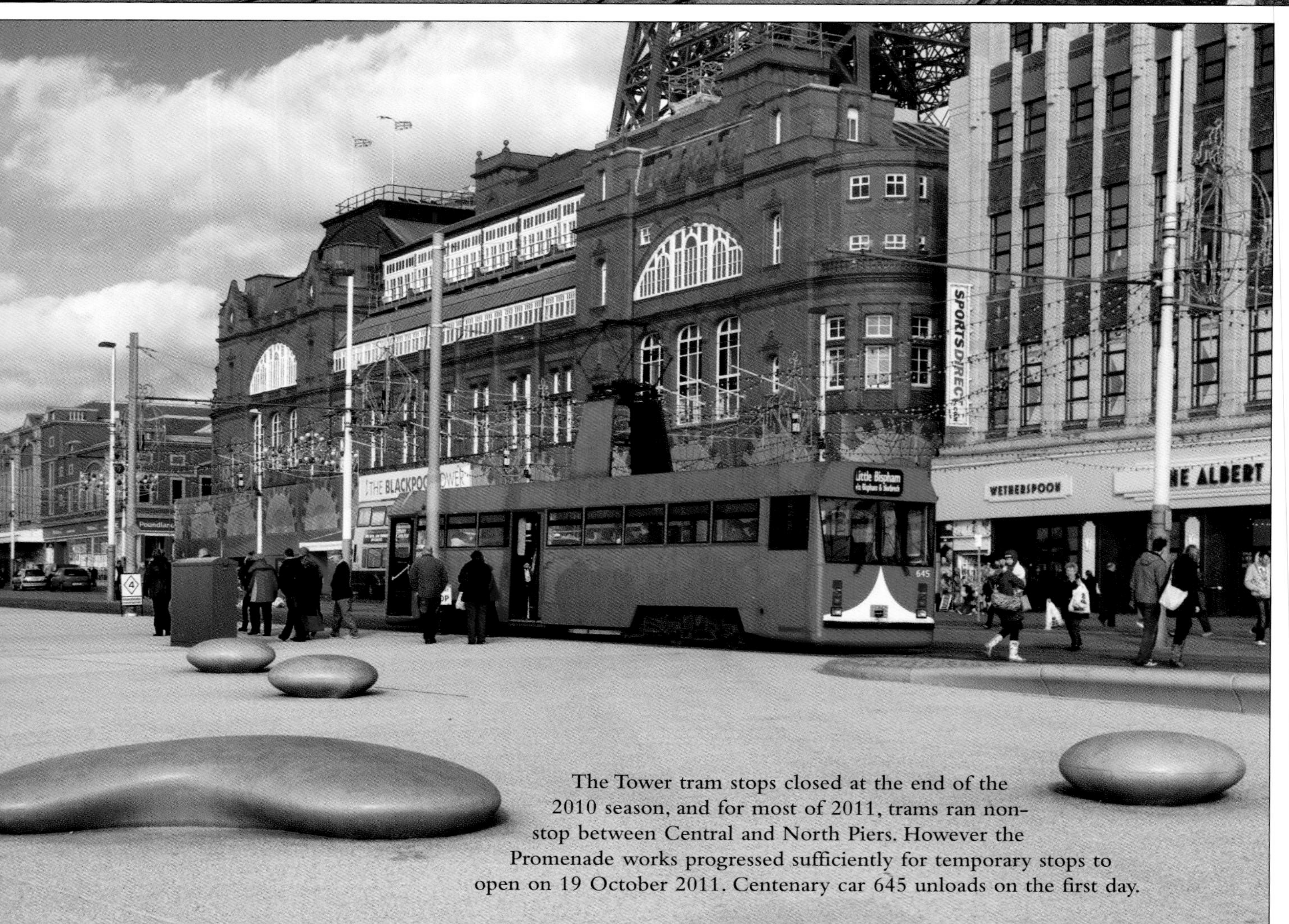

The Tower tram stops closed at the end of the 2010 season, and for most of 2011, trams ran non-stop between Central and North Piers. However the Promenade works progressed sufficiently for temporary stops to open on 19 October 2011. Centenary car 645 unloads on the first day.

Southbound Stops

Until 1961 there were two southbound shelters at the Tower - one for the Promenade, and the other for the Lytham Road route to Squire's Gate.

Right The Squire's Gate shelter, being some way south of the Tower, rarely appears on photographs. Standard car 49 is passing in August 1961, having loaded at the Promenade stop. The sign *Watson Rd. for Pleasure Beach* was added in 1958 to lure gullible visitors away from the busy Promenade cars. It was not well received, either by Lytham Road regulars - who said their trams were full enough already - or by visitors who found themselves facing a long walk at the other end. The shelter was removed after the Squire's Gate route closed on 29 October 1961.

A view from the open balcony of Standard car 40 in 1961. On the left is the old northbound stop and on the right the southbound Promenade shelter.

Southbound Stops

Top The south end of the Promenade shelter, probably in 1962, with Boat 225 passing Standard car 147. (*Malcolm King collection*)

Centre In 1972 the steel shelter was replaced by a home-built wooden model, similar to the southbound shelters at North Pier and the Cabin. On the left the old Rowell shelter had become such a popular feature that when the Promenade cast-iron shelters gave way to Adshels in 1972, it too was replaced by an Adshel, bearing a sign *This Shelter is not a Tram Stop*. OMO 4 passes on 17 April 1973. (*Peter Makinson*)

Below The southern end of the wooden shelter, with Coronation 660 - the last of its class still running - in October 1981.

Southbound Stops

Above In 1986 the southbound shelter was refurbished, and its direction reversed. Passengers seem to be making heavy weather of boarding experimental Centenary 651 on 24 August 1986.

Centre To mark the centenary of the Tower in 1994, the Promenade between there and North Pier was given a 'heritage' look. The four tram shelters on this stretch, including the southbound one at the Tower, were replaced. Boat 605 edges past the half-built shelter on 1 May 1994.

Bottom The heritage shelter on 5 June 2005, with Balloon 724 - the last of four cars (707, 709, 718 and 724) rebuilt with twin-car style fronts between 1998 and 2004.

Southbound Stops

Left The southbound heritage shelter at the Tower was removed with the three-track layout after the 2009 season. On 9 October 2010, Coronation 660 loads at an unfamiliar-looking stop; no shelter, no bridge and for the first time in 34 years it's possible to get tram and Tower in the same picture. The Tower, incidentally, is Blackpool's only Grade I listed building.

Below The Tower tram stops were closed for most of 2011 whilst the Supertram platforms were built on (and opposite) the site of the old southbound stop. Balloon 717 - running non-stop between Central and North Piers - passes the construction work on 28 June 2011.

Southbound Stops

Top The southbound Supertram platform and shelter were finished by October 2011, to the confusion of would-be passengers, who waited there, only for the tram to sail straight past them. Centenary 647 observes this great Blackpool tradition on 7 October.

Centre For a couple of weeks from 19 October 2011 a temporary southbound stop was in use, to the north of the Supertram platform. Centenary 642 arrives on 5 November.

Below In bad weather, canny passengers waited in the shelter before walking up to the temporary stop, though this required some poor soul to stand there in the first place. Centenary 645 on a breezy 19 October, the stop's first day.

Supertram Stops

Above On 11 July 2013, Flexity 002 arrives at the southbound shelter, which is enclosed on all four sides. Much of the glass has since been replaced by advertising panels (which may have been the intention all along, this being a prime location) and the shelter is now almost as claustrophobic as the narrow heritage shelter used to be.

Below The Supertram platforms are in the same positions as the Promenade tram stops were before 1962. Northbound Flexity 011 loads on 11 July 2013, with the southbound shelter still displaying the re-opening poster from April 2012.

3. Stops for the Shops

Victoria Street and Church Street

In days gone by, tram stops came thick and fast after leaving the Tower. In 1903 there were eight between there and Pleasant Street - a distance of about 1,000 yards. This had been reduced to five by 1960. Now there's just one.

Above Victoria Street was the first stop after the Tower - so close, in fact, that if you missed a tram at the Tower, you could catch it at Victoria Street. Rebuilt Balloon No. 724 loads at the southbound stop on 26 September 2008, in front of the Woolworths store - formerly Lewis's, and before that the Palace entertainment complex.

Victoria Street

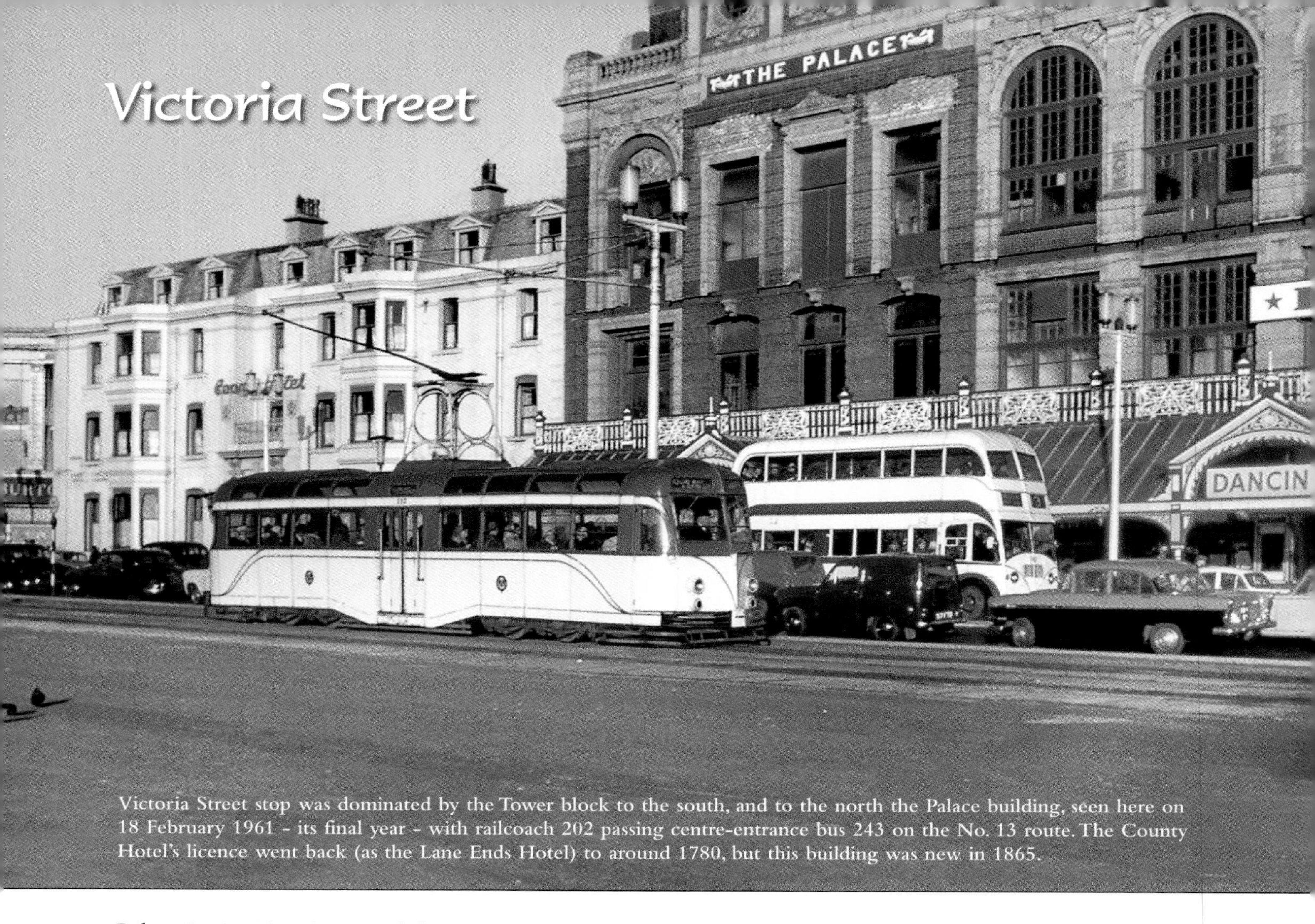

Victoria Street stop was dominated by the Tower block to the south, and to the north the Palace building, seen here on 18 February 1961 - its final year - with railcoach 202 passing centre-entrance bus 243 on the No. 13 route. The County Hotel's licence went back (as the Lane Ends Hotel) to around 1780, but this building was new in 1865.

Below Passing Victoria Street shelter in the Autumn of 1961 is twin-car 275/T5, bearing the short-lived (and usually mis-set) boards listing the twin-cars' limited stops, which surprisingly included Victoria Street. No. 275 - last seen (*page 17*) as a trailer behind No. 276 - was converted back to a motor car in 1961. (*Marcus Eavis/On-line Transport Archive*)

Victoria Street

Right The Palace and the adjoining County Hotel were demolished in 1962 and replaced by Lewis's store, with its honeycombed facade. Brush car 624 calls at Victoria Street's cast-iron shelter on 23 October 1971. Neither would serve the public much longer. The shelter was replaced by an Adshel during the following winter, while 624 was withdrawn a few days later to become a Permanent Way car, with the same fleet number. It became 748 in April 1985 and 259 in November 1986 when the permanent way fleet passed from Blackpool Transport to the Council after de-regulation.

In 1975 'Coffin' car 618 heads for Victoria Street's Adshel, where OMO car 9 is loading at the southbound stop. No. 618 was withdrawn in October 1975 and reappeared as OMO 13 in June 1976.

Victoria Street

Top Victoria Street in winter. Northbound OMO car 5 - with experimental Brecknell Willis high-reach pantograph - picks up Christmas shoppers at Victoria Street's Adshel during relaying of the east track in December 1981.

Centre Victoria Street at Easter. On 11 April 1998, Balloon 722 calls at the attractive heritage shelter which replaced the Adshel as part of the refurbishment of the Promenade in 1994 - the same year that Lewis's store was rebuilt with two less storeys, and taken over by Woolworths.

Below Victoria Street in high season. Wall's Ice Cream tram, No. 719, sails past the southbound queue at Victoria Street on 31 July 1999, leaving passengers to take their chance on 703.

Coronation 304 loads at Victoria Street's heritage shelter in the twilight on 5 November 2006.

Centenary car 645 leaves the southbound stop on 12 August 2010. The Promenade works are engulfing the Victoria Street stop, and it disappeared at the end of that season, after serving for exactly 100 years.

Farewell, Victoria Street

Above Not much interest from Newcastle United - less still from Liverpool - in the defunct Victoria Street stop, which southbound 647 has just passed on 20 June 2011. The notice in the cab warns drivers of Centenary cars not to take the south curve at the Pleasure Beach unless an inspector is present.

Below Hard to credit that this lunar landscape is normally the busiest part of the Promenade. Balloon 719 - running non-stop from Central Pier between security fencing on 23 April 2011 - passes the site of the Victoria Street stop. At the left, work has started on laying the Comedy Carpet (*see page 14*).

Victoria Street to Church Street

Top Return of the red tram. Forty years after disappearing as a fleet livery, red re-appeared on OMO car 10, seen between Victoria Street and Church Street on 3 May 1975, two months after entering service. (*Peter Makinson*)

Bottom Rebuilt Balloon 718 - in Metro Coastlines Line 3 blue and yellow - approaches Church Street on 22 August 2008, with the Lancashire Constabulary's mounted patrol receiving most of the attention.

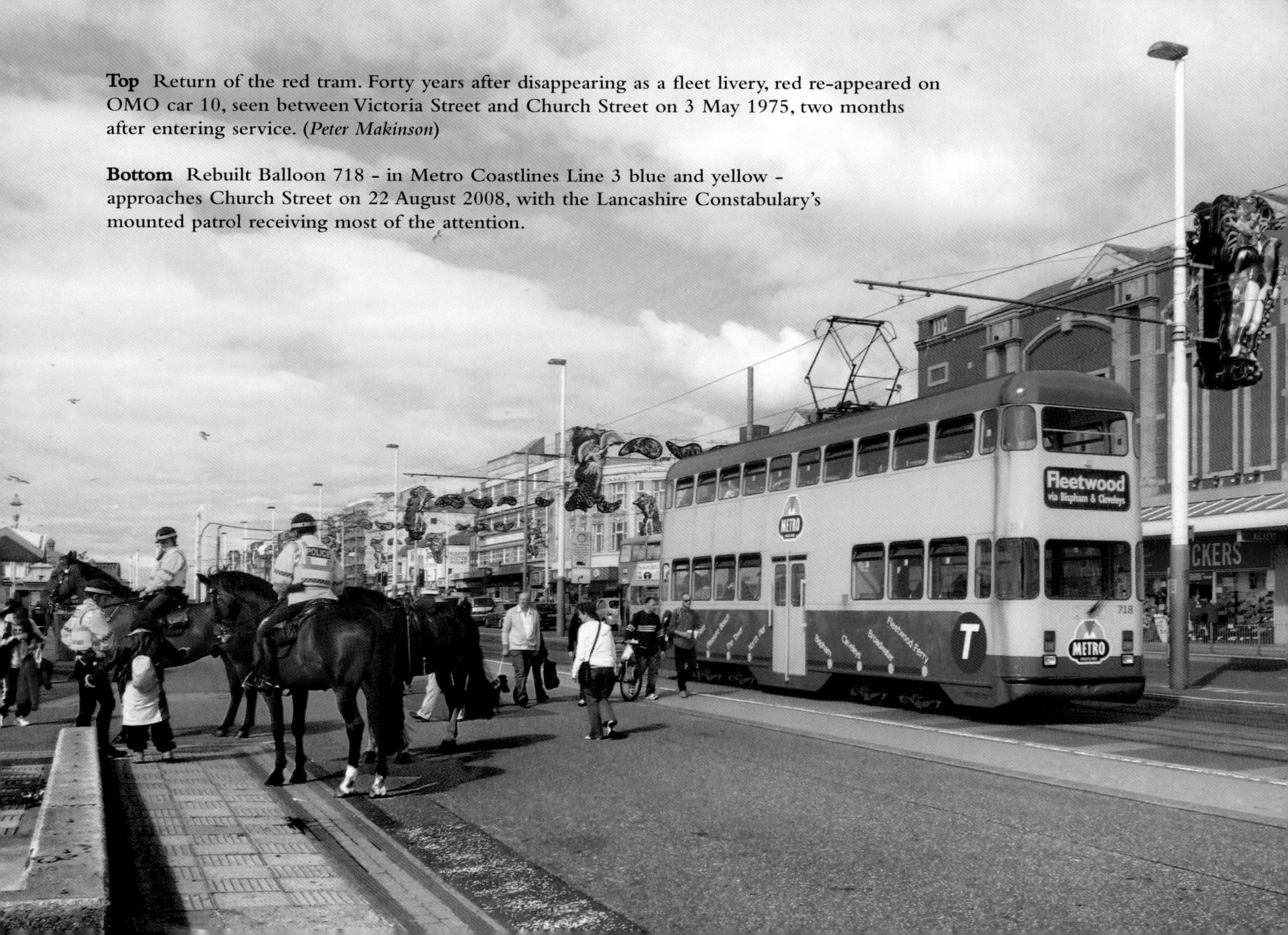

The Changing Scene

Above Standard car 147 in August 1961, seen from the open balcony of sister car 40. No. 147 was sold to an Ohio trolley museum in 1967 for £50. Passing the County Hotel is centre-entrance bus 256 on its way to South Pier via the former Central Drive tram route. In the background the northbound Church Street stop is still in use.

Same tram, same place on 13 July 2003. No. 147 came home in October 2000, exchanged for Boat car 606.

Church Street

Top Church Street tram stop achieved celluloid immortality in 1934 with an encounter between a railcoach and a cycling Gracie Fields. Filming of *Sing As We Go* disrupted the tram service from 1.30 to 2.45 on 31 May 1934.

Centre The northbound stop received a cast-iron shelter in April 1924. Although it ceased to be a tram stop in March 1964, the shelter remained for communal use. Coronation 311 passes in 1965.

Below The southbound stop was removed in 1942. Looking north from the site of the old stop on 5 August 1961, all four cars - Coronation 324, Balloon 249 and Standards 49 and 147 - survive.

Not a Tram Stop

Above Church Street's communal (ex-tramway) cast-iron shelter - like that at the Tower - was replaced in January 1972 by an Adshel bearing a notice *This Shelter is not a Tram Stop*. OMO car 10 passes the Adshel on 3 May 1975. (*Peter Makinson*)

Centre OMO 13 in January 1980, with the shelter on borrowed time. Drivers complained that passengers still waited there and stepped in front of the tram to stop it, so the Adshel was removed in October 1980. (*Alan Spencer collection*)

Bottom (left) Brush car 633 - the Post Office tram - passes the site of the Adshel in August 1983.

Bottom (right) The interior of 633, with Post Office clerk and letter box.

4. North Pier

North Pier was the heart of the old Blackpool tramway and - to a lesser extent - is still the centre of the Supertram system. This chapter covers North Pier in general, while Chapter 5 looks at the tram stops.

Above On 19 April 2014, twin-car 272/T2 loads at the northbound heritage stop on the latest North Pier siding (*see page 55*).

End of the Marton Link

Until 1963 there was a single-track junction between the Marton terminus in Talbot Square and the Promenade route at North Pier. It was used by Boats on the Circular Tour, and by cars from Marton Depot working special Promenade duties. The link carried fare-paying passengers for the last time on 11 September 1960, when the final Circular Tour ran.

Top The illuminated Gondola waits to follow the *Blackpool Belle* over the single-track, heading to Marton Depot for storage on 7 August 1962. In front of them the Rocket suffers the indignity of being towed backwards by a Boat. (*Malcolm King collection*)

Centre The penultimate use of the connecting line came on 11 March 1963, when a convoy of three cars (Balloon 251, the partly dismantled Gondola, and Standard car 48) moved back from Marton Depot to Rigby Road. (*E.C. Bennett/On-line Transport Archive*)

The link was last used on 31 May 1963, when the Western Train ran up Church Street for the opening of the ABC Cinema. Four days later, the overhead was removed. The connecting track into Talbot Square remained until traffic lights were installed at the junction, a few weeks after Brush car 292 passed on 25 February 1967.

Works Cars at North Pier

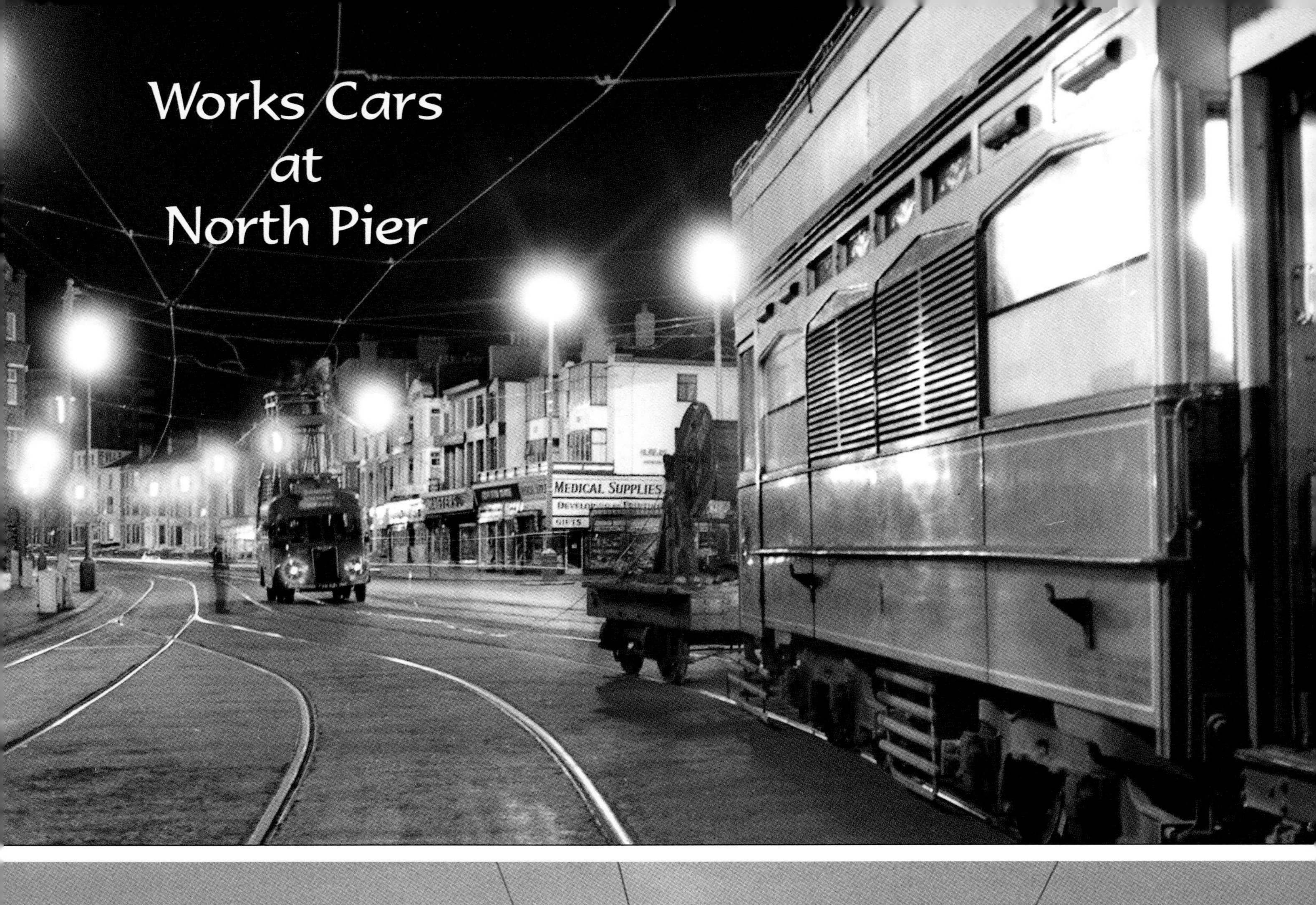

Top In the small hours of 18 May 1966, works car 3 is reversing and playing out copper wire from the former Tramroad reel wagon, while the crew on ex-Manchester Guy tower wagon No. 240 fix the new wire in place.

Bottom In November 1981, OMO car 1 passes gang car 624 and PW Bus 437.

North Pier in the Snow

Above OMO 12 has run to the limit of the southbound track to allow car No. 1 behind to reverse on 15 December 1981. Trams were only running between North Pier and Ash Street, the remaining tracks still being blocked by the previous day's snowfall.

Below On 19 December 1981, Brush car 634 and Balloon 701 (coupled together) are shuttling between North Pier and Pleasure Beach to keep the tracks free of ice. OMO 4 reverses in the background.

Tour of Illuminations

Above In the early 1960s the Tour of Illuminations moved from the Tower to North Pier, where it loaded on the centre track. In October 1985, Standard car 40 waits for switch-on, with Jubilee 762 behind.

Below The Lights are on, No. 40 has gone, and 762 is loading for the next tour.

The Centenary Siding

In March 1985 a siding was laid at North Pier to display cars visiting Blackpool for the Tramway Centenary. A different car was on show each day. As the siding had no overhead wire, the day's exhibit was shunted onto the siding early each morning, usually by the Unimog tower wagon, but sometimes by works car 748, pushing crane car 751 to give the required length.

Top Two high-capacity double-deckers - Dreadnought 59 of 1902 on the siding in July 1985, alongside Jubilee 762 (the very last of the breed), built eighty years later.

Centre Three abreast - Manchester 765 is tramcar *du jour*, with OMO 8 and Dreadnought 59 again, on 2 June.

Below And four - Glasgow 1297 on display, with OMO 7, Pantograph 167 and Coronation 660 occupying the other three tracks on 22 June.

The Centenary Siding

Above On Centenary day, 29 September 1985, the Mayor unveils the Centenary plaque - a Measured Mile post from Lytham Road. The absence of wires doesn't bother the National Tramway Museum's steam tram *John Bull,* celebrating its own 100th birthday. (*Peter Fitton*)

Centre On 13 July 1985 John Markham of GEC Traction presents 651's controller handle to Coun. Stanley Parkinson, Transportation Committee Chairman, who is holding the original controller handle used on conduit car 5 at the opening ceremony on 29 September 1885. Conduit car No. 4 stands on the points leading to the siding. (*Peter Makinson*)

Bottom An overall view of Princess Parade, the Metropole Hotel and the four-track layout on 2 June 1985.

A Dying Art

Above Blackpool is one of only seven tramways - all tourist-oriented - in the world where trolley poles are still turned, though nowadays it only happens during heritage operations. On 27 September 2008, Boat 600's guard performs what was still an everyday summer ritual, though always something of a spectator sport.

Below (left) On 5 September 1998, Fleetwood Box car 40's guard demonstrates the art with a trolley rope. Fleetwood cars traditionally used ropes, Blackpool cars bamboo poles.

Below (right) One of each needed to turn the Western Train's trolley on 17 June 2010.

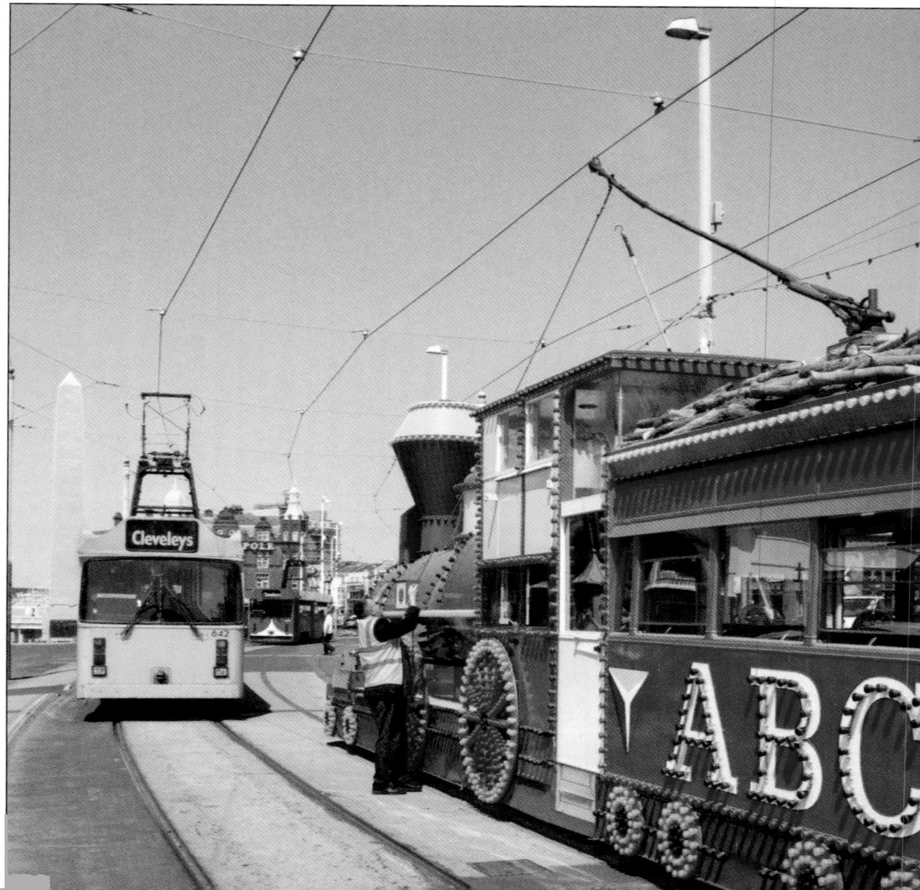

North Pier's Own Tramway

From 1991 to 2003 a three-car diesel-hydraulic tram-set ran on a 250 yard long line along North Pier, laid to a gauge of 2ft. 11in. The vehicles - built by Harry Steer Engineering of Breaston, Derbyshire - were lifted onto the pier by crane from the sands.

Above Two forms of transport on North Pier in September 1991. The tram - in its first month of operation - has just left the seaward terminus at the new Carousel Bar, while the JetRanger helicopter has taken off from the jetty for a trip to South Shore and back.

Centre The tram-train at the Carousel Bar terminus in September 1991. The red colour scheme was chosen from the standard shades available for the fibreglass from which the body was built.

Bottom The inland terminus on 24 July 2012. The tramway closed in November 2003, and the cars were broken up at Jacksons' yard in Marton during June 2004.

All Dressed Up

Illuminated Cars at North Pier

All Dressed Up

Above The Rocket, No. 732 - here waiting for the nightly switch-on at North Pier in September 1981 - was constructed in 1961 on the underframe of Pantograph car 168.

Below Ahead of 732 in the queue is No. 736, *HMS Blackpool*, with the Western Train and Bolton 66 behind. No. 736 was based on the remains of Pantograph 170 in 1965.

Opposite A party waiting outside North Pier to board the Hovertram on 5 September 1998. No. 735 was built in 1963 on the frame of railcoach 222.

All Dressed Up

Top These boards were placed on the west side of the northbound shelter each night. Seen here in October 1981.

Centre Like the Dreadnoughts of old, most of the illuminated cars loaded at the rear - a potentially lethal arrangement with service cars overtaking on the outside track. *HMS Blackpool's* conductor keeps a wary eye open for approaching trams on 26 September 1998.

Below For forty years and more, the Tour of Illuminations loaded on the centre track at North Pier. This is No. 735, the Hovertram, on 12 September 1983.

All Dressed Up

Above *HMS Blackpool* was heavily rebuilt for the 2004 Illuminations. It is seen at North Pier alongside Bolton 66 on 18 September that year.

Centre The Western Train ready to depart on 5 September 1998. The Train was built in 1962, using railcoach 209 for the locomotive and Pantograph 174 for the carriage. The hoses and couplings were spare when the original programme for twelve twin-cars was reduced to ten.

Bottom The Western Train was restored with Lottery funding in 2009. The locomotive was transferred to the frame of twin-car 677, and fitted with a wheelchair lift. To accommodate this, the long-standing arrangements at North Pier were reversed, so that Tour cars loaded on the western track, with service cars overtaking on the centre line. Wheelchair-bound passengers are taken aboard the locomotive on 26 September 2009.

Beset by Buses

During the last years of the old layout at North Pier, the path of northbound trams was regularly blocked by Line 1 buses loading at their singularly ill-placed stop by the cenotaph.

Above Restored Balloon 717 waits patiently - or not - on 16 August 2010, while ex-Trent Olympian No. 403 loads slowly at the Line 1 stop.

Centre Stuck behind a Line 6 Delta, Jubilee car 762 also has Solo No. 287 and Trident 324 snapping at its heels. Things weren't normally quite so chaotic, but this was 16 February 2009, the morning after Yates's Wine Lodge burned down. Talbot Square was closed to traffic, and all bus services diverted via the Metropole.

Bottom On 3 July 2008, Centenary car 646 waits for ex-Blackburn Trident 335, which Balloon 723 has just managed to squeeze past.

End of the Old Layout

Above The three-track layout lasted until the end of the 2010 season, which also saw the 125th anniversary of the opening of the Promenade tramway on 29 September 1885. Twin-car 681/671 passes the entrance to North Pier on 11 September 2010.

Below Pantograph 170, Standard 147 and ex-Tramroad car 40 bring a pre-war look to North Pier on the same unsettled afternoon. These three cars may just have met here between 1934 and 1937, though only when the Pantograph was going to or from depot.

End of the Old Layout

Above Single-deckers of varying heights at North Pier on 3 September 2010 - trailer car 685, Boat 602, and Oporto 273 (on a test run).

Below The guard enjoys the time-honoured cigarette as Sheffield 513 reverses in the rain on 26 October 2010. The four-wheeler rarely operated in service after derailing on the Tramroad in May 2003 (*see page 159*). 513 ran for the last time five days later, before leaving for the East Anglia Transport Museum.

The New Siding

In place of the old three-track layout, the new tramway incorporated a siding between West Street and Church Street, with crossovers north and south of it. The siding didn't find a regular purpose until the 2011 Illuminations started in September (*see page 56*).

Right On 30 July 2011, Balloon 718 waits at the *Halt* signs as another widened car, No. 713, reverses on the northern crossover. The first of these nine *B Fleet* Balloons - adapted to use the Supertram platforms - entered service on 14 July 2011.

Below For most of the 2011 season, the new siding was used for parking spare cars - in this case widened Balloon 720. Overtaking No. 720 on 13 August 2011 is twin-car 685/675 in its final season. As No. 275, 675 had been the trailer of the prototype twin-car in 1958 (*see page 17*).

Christening the Siding

The first regular operational use of the new siding was to load the Tour of Illuminations, whose traditional departure point on the three-track layout had disappeared. Because the unfinished Promenade works left no space for cars to load from the seaward side of the siding, special arrangements were made, as shown here on 24 September 2011.

Above Passengers queue at a yellow Tour stop on the new southbound Supertram platform. At 7.27 p.m. the Western Train arrives on the siding for the first tour of the evening.

Centre By 7.58 the Train has long departed, and the next tour car, the Trawler, is already full. Passengers wait to be shepherded across the tracks by an inspector. The Trawler was built in 2001, using Brush car 633.

Bottom At 8.05 the Trawler has left, and passengers are boarding Standard car 147 by the front platform.

Although the new siding (and heritage stop) seem eminently suited to the task, all Tour cars now load at the Pleasure Beach, which offers better car parking.

North Pier's Aerial Ballet

Above At dusk as many as 20,000 starlings - officially a 'murmuration' - gather from all over the Fylde to swirl spectacularly in the skies around North Pier. Just a small part of the aerial ballet above Flexity 015 on 27 November 2012.

Below (left) On 21 November 2012, birds *en route* from St Annes take a rest on the wires at Starr Gate above Flexity 009.

Below (right) Starlings swoop over Olympian 403 at the Line 1 bus stop on 17 January 2009.

4. North Pier Tram Stops

Unloading Only

Over the years, Blackpool's *Unloading Only* stops shrank from these large wooden boards to the insignificant blue diamond which Brush car 622 is approaching (*opposite*) on 18 April 2009.

Above Coronation 316 unloads on 1 January 1962 - the second coldest day (11°F) then recorded in Blackpool. Behind 316 are the northbound cast-iron shelters at Church Street and Victoria Street, and on the left the southbound shelters for the Promenade and Lytham Road.

Below Twin-car 277/T7 passes reversible set 281/T1 by the southbound unloading stop in August 1965. The stop had been moved further south when the Marton route closed.

Southbound Stops 1961

Above There were two southbound steel shelters at North Pier. Standard car No. 147 has loaded at the Promenade stop and is accelerating past the Squire's Gate shelter in August 1961.

Below Railcoach 217, having arrived from Squire's Gate, is reversing on the south crossover before returning to Rigby Road depot in October 1961. Promenade cars reversing at North Pier had to use the north crossover to reach their shelter. When the Lytham Road closed at the end of that month, the Promenade shelter was removed and all cars used the former Squire's Gate shelter. (*Charles Benson*)

Wooden Shelter 1972

In 1972 the steel shelter, which dated from 1942, was replaced by a wooden one made at Rigby Road. It was painted this vague beige colour, rather than the traditional green and cream.

Above On 6 October 1973 Brush car 638 - in contrast to the shelter - had just received green and cream in place of the all-cream livery it wore as the one-man prototype. (*Peter Makinson*)

Below Jubilee 761 pulls away from the wooden shelter in July 1981.

Back to Green

Top In January 1992 the wooden shelter was painted a rather odd shade of green, not quite matching recently overhauled towing car 680, seen here in June that year.

Centre The green shelter lasted only two years before being replaced by a heritage design (as at the Tower and Victoria Street) in 1994. Loading there in July 1995 is towing car 679, newly repainted - but not yet lettered - to advertise the associated Seagull Coaches operation.

Below On 11 September 2010, Balloon 726 passes the narrow shelter alongside an equally cramped Promenade before reversing. Quite why Her Majesty's Coastguard needed to advertise was never made clear.

A Brief Stop

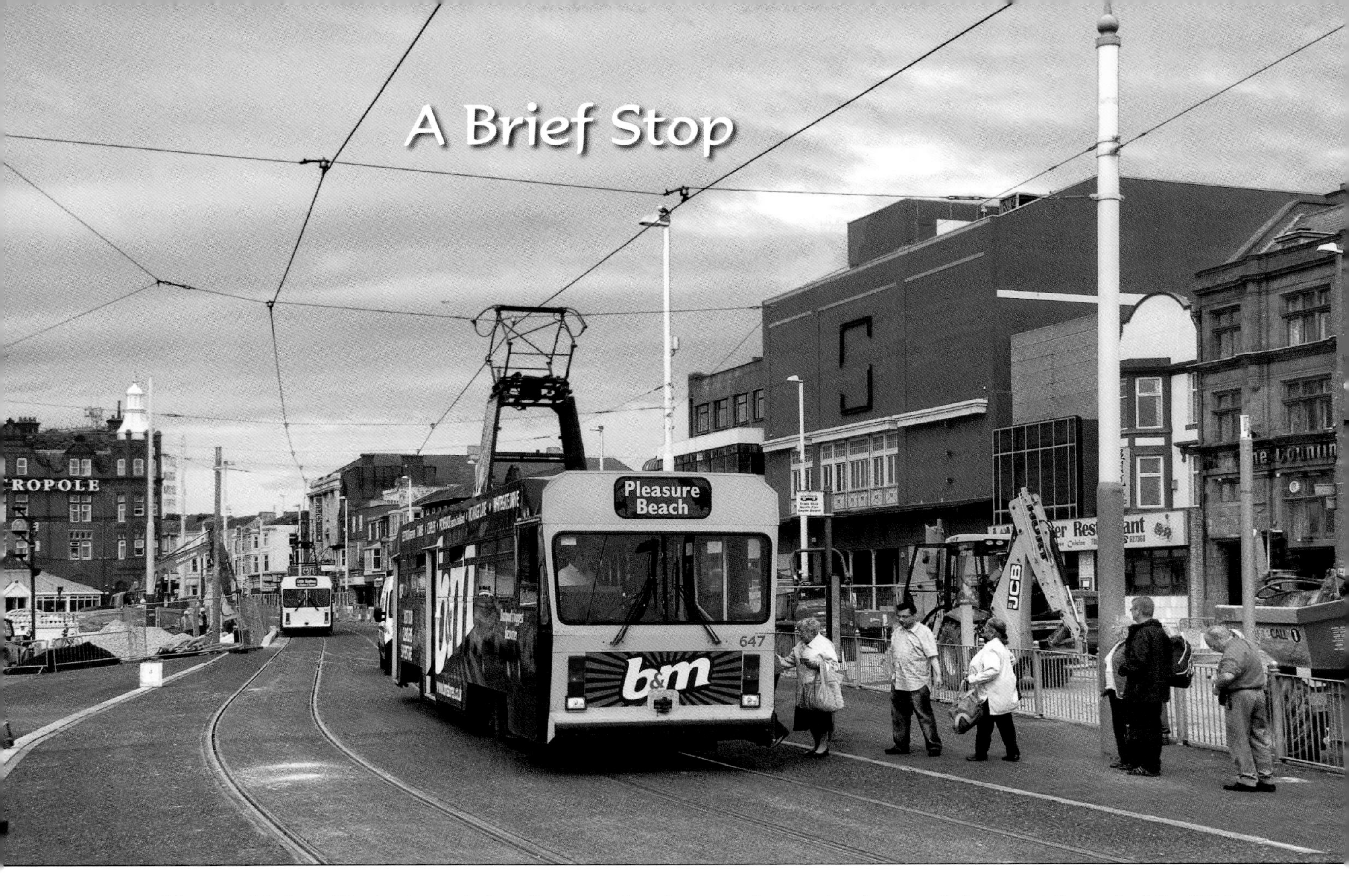

Above and below The heritage shelter disappeared at the same time as the three-track layout, at the end of the 2010 season. When the tramway reopened as far as North Pier on 22 April 2011, there was no southbound stop, since all cars reversed and loaded on the northbound track (*see page 78*). Once the service was extended to Uncle Tom's Cabin on 6 May, a new southbound stop was introduced, about 100 yards north of the traditional position. Centenary 647 loads at the 2011-style sign on 15 June, three days before the end of the stop's six-week life.

Church Street Reborn

On 18 June 2011, the southbound stop moved once more, this time almost two hundred yards, right down to Church Street - nearly seventy years after the old southbound stop there was discontinued in 1942.

Above Twin-car 675/685 loads on 18 June 2011 at a temporary stop in front of the half-built Festival House - an eclectic building comprising cafe, tourist information bureau and wedding chapel.

On 18 June 2011 Balloon 717 approaches the re-located southbound stop at Church Street, with its distinctly non-standard stop sign.

Church Street Reborn

On 21 June 2011 the peripatetic southbound stop at Church Street was moved one pole further south, and upgraded to a fully-fledged tram stop with the latest style of sign. This remained in use until 1 November; for the last five days of the old system, trams used a temporary stop slightly further north (*see page 67*).

Above The general layout on 5 August 2011, with Centenary 648 standing just short of the stop (the pole with the yellow notice) and Optare Solo No. 249 emerging from Church Street on route 5.

Below Centenary 642 passes Boat 600 as it waits at the 2011 Church Street stop on 30 September.

Southbound Supertram Stop

Top While the tram stops were moving to and fro during 2011, the southbound Supertram platform was under construction opposite West Street. On Easter Saturday, 23 April, Balloon 715 passes the platform in its early stages. No. 715 ran in this Metro Coastlines Line 16 livery (which it received in 2008) for only a few days in 2011, before being repainted into 1970s-style green and cream (*see opposite*).

Centre Unloading the Trueform Elite shelter on 31 August.

Below Early in September the platform received its stylish new name-board, or rather it mistakenly received one intended for the Tower. No. 631 goes north on 22 September; 631 and 632 were the only Brush cars running in 2011.

The completed platform on 19 October 2011. Balloon 717 waits for a school party, while 715 is on the popular Tram Driving Experience, which offered members of the public a day's tram driving for £350.

From 2 November 2011 the southbound stop at Church Street was replaced by a temporary stop on the site of the old shelter, just north of the Tour of Illuminations stop. Brush car 632 is about to reverse on the stop's first day.

Southbound Supertram Stop

Above The Supertram platform is almost as far south as the old Church Street stop, and well placed for the town centre. Flexity 001 disgorges a crowd of shoppers on 16 April 2012.

Below Flexity 006 unloads at the southbound stop on 4 September 2013. In the background is some of the oldest property on the Promenade, including the 200-year-old Oyster Rooms at the corner of West Street.

Waiting for the bride - a landau horse in all its finery stands patiently outside the Festival House wedding chapel on 30 June 2012. Flexity 003 waits at the southbound tram stop, though not for the bride.

Below As at the Tower, the southbound Trueform shelter at North Pier is enclosed on all four sides. Flexity 012 arrives on 14 May 2012.

Heritage Stops

The northbound heritage stop is on the new siding. On 2 August 2012, Standard car 147 is being filmed for a travelogue programme with Rory Bremner.

Balloon 717 leaves the stop on 19 April 2014. Northbound heritage cars generally load on the siding, but sometimes use the centre track.

Heritage Stops

Above Although the resurrected Church Street stop vanished again in November 2011, it reappeared in 2012 as the southbound heritage tram stop. Brush car 631 departs on 14 July 2012. Since this picture was taken, 631 has been repainted green and cream.

Centre Bolton 66 attracts attention at the heritage stop - by the rarely-used southern crossover - on 19 April 2014.

Bottom Newly restored twin-car 272/T2 calls at Church Street on the evening of 14 September 2012.

North Pier's Double Shelter

From 1942 to 1991, northbound passengers used a long steel shelter, divided into two sections, originally intended to cope with heavy wartime demand from billeted troops and civil servants requisitioned in the North Shore hotels.

Above Standard car 147 reverses, while a Balloon loads for Cabin at the southern section - for cars going as far as Bispham. Some long-standing Blackpool traders appear on the right - the UCP restaurant, E.H. Booth (grocers), Thomas Nutbrown (kitchen appliances) and photographer H.E. Howarth, who sold colour slides of the trams.

Below (left) A close-up of the illuminated sign, with other typical Blackpool tram-stop appurtenances.

Below (right) The shelter and the third track dated from May 1942. Originally the short-haul and long-haul sections were the other way round, as seen here with railcoach 273 in 1952. Between the two sections was a small inspector's cabin.

North Pier's Double Shelter

Above The shelter in October 1961, with car 319 on the Starr Gate to Thornton Gate service. During that season, the Coronations carried road safety slogans in their trolley towers. (*Charles Benson*)

Centre In 1969/70 the layout of the shelter was altered so that the two queues faced south instead of north. The illuminated stop signs remained, but were re-positioned. The duty inspector chats to the driver of a Brush car waiting for Coronation 656 (ex-320) to load at the Fleetwood portion of the shelter on 15 July 1971.

Bottom For the OMO implementation in 1972, the northern half of the shelter was closed off and all cars used the southern part. A painted notice was mounted over the southern end of the shelter, seen here in 1975 with Balloon 702 passing.

North Pier's Double Shelter

Above OMO car 8 loads at the shelter on 3 June 1978.

Centre Early in 1979 the southernmost section of the structure was rebuilt for the inspector's use (replacing the central cabin) as seen here with Coronation 660 on the evening of 9 September 1985. The remainder was made into one long south-facing shelter.

Bottom The north end wasn't often photographed. Towing car 679 loads on the centre track in June 1987.

Opposite (top) When the shelter was built in 1942, the Transport Committee promised to remove it after the war if it was thought to be unsightly; it lasted, in fact, until 1991. Its replacement, an aluminium structure by Commutaports of Glasgow, appeared in August that year. Twin-car 673/683 loads on 24 August 1997.

Opposite (bottom) The northern end of the 1991 shelter, with Centenary 644 on 7 November 2005, while the north crossover was being removed.

The Commutaports Shelter

Displaced by Royalty

On 28 June 2008 the Duchess of Cornwall named Boat 600 after herself in a ceremony by the cenotaph. To clear a space for the event, the Commutaports shelter was demolished, and the stop moved south to where the unloading stop had been. On 21 October 2008, P.W. bus 950 stands by as 719 loads.

Below The cause of all the trouble - Boat 600, now *Duchess of Cornwall* - alongside Balloon 723 loading at the stop on 27 September 2008. 723's 1980s-style colour scheme is really an advertising livery for Automedon, who took over the former TVR sports-car factory at Bispham in 2006.

Trueform Shelter

Top A Trueform Elite shelter appeared in November 2008 but wasn't used until January 2009. Centenary 646 on 4 November 2009.

Bottom Twin-car 671/681 on 23 October 2010, two weeks before the shelter was used for the last time.

The End of the Line

Top During the winter of 2010/11 the tramway, the carriageway and the Promenade itself were all being rebuilt. The tram service restarted on 22 April for Easter, but only between Pleasure Beach and North Pier, where Brush car 632 reverses on 29 April amidst a maze of barriers and security fencing.

Bottom Balloon 717 on 23 April 2011. There wasn't a tram stop as such, apart from the yellow sign shown opposite.

New Tracks, Old Trams

Above On 6 May 2011 the tram service was extended to Uncle Tom's Cabin, and the temporary terminus at North Pier became the northbound stop. It was graced with a new style of sign - with slightly eccentric wording - which appeared at several stops during April 2011. The North Pier stop also featured this unique yellow sign. Centenary car 645 is loading on 6 October 2011.

Centre The tram service was further extended from Cabin to Little Bispham on 27 May 2011. Newly repainted Balloon 715 calls at the stop on 28 June.

Bottom 715's passengers need a helping hand. Compared to the Centenary cars, the steps on the centre-entrance cars were daunting for some.

Centenary Swansong

Above By 26 September 2011, the northbound Supertram platform and shelter were almost finished. Centenary 645 gives a passable impression of a traffic cone.

Below Next stop, Central Pier. On 13 May 2011 Centenary 646 leaves North Pier between the work-sites for rebuilding the Promenade and the carriageway.

Supertram Stop

The Supertram platform, which opened on 4 April 2012, was even further north than the old northbound stop. Flexity 003 loads there under a mackerel sky on 22 September 2012, with competing RM 1568 at the bus stop - now relocated out of harm's way.

The new layout made short-workings to North Pier possible, but problematical. No. 700's driver has re-set his headlights and is ready to reverse on 4 May 2013. Just as the photograph was taken, a northbound Flexity appeared round the curve by the pier, blocking the path to the distant crossover near the new siding and forcing 700 to scuttle off north to the next reversing place - a mile and a half away at Uncle Tom's Cabin.

6. Behind the Metropole

The Metropole is Blackpool's oldest hotel - dating back to 1776 - and was the best in town until the Imperial opened in 1867. The hotel's unique position right on the shore-line was jealously guarded by the owners, who refused to let the local authority extend the promenade round the front of their property in 1866. So the tramway (when it was built in 1885) had to run behind the hotel and - despite numerous schemes to divert it - still does.

Above Towing car 679 disappears into the mist behind the Metropole on 29 November 2008 - fitting weather for the tram's farewell run before it was withdrawn for preservation.

Standard car 49 forces its way through the traffic on 5 August 1961. A 1951 Humber Super Snipe and a Vauxhall Victor follow new trailer car T6 behind the Metropole.

The Early Sixties

Centre In August 1961 Standard car 160 passes the new Regent Court flats, and edges round the north corner of the Metropole. *Tram Pinch* signs were introduced by the Ministry of Transport in 1934, but this one wasn't erected until the 1950s. In 1965, when new standard designs appeared (not including *Tram Pinch*), this sign was given special dispensation to remain, but was struck by a car in 1970 and never replaced.

Bottom Until April 1962 there was a rather obscure tram stop behind the hotel, patronised by a few regular passengers, and known to the Transport Department as *Metropole* (northbound) and *Princess Cinema* (southbound). The southbound stop was made unloading-only in 1943, and wasn't used at all when the Illuminations were on. In January 1962, a rare passenger has flagged down towing car 277, working wrong-line during trackwork near the hotel entrance (*see next page*).

Metropole Layout 1962

The top end of the three-track layout outside North Pier was altered early in 1962 to give a straight run north for cars on the loop line. These two photographs show the short (and short-lived) shuttle between North Pier and Bispham, which replaced part of the Squire's Gate - Bispham tram service. As with other Blackpool shuttles, cars showed both destinations, to save crews having to change four blinds every few minutes.

Above Railcoach 203 leaves the centre track, while the new alignment for the loop line takes shape.

Below In a simpler world - before traffic cones and security fencing - a Brush car takes the new track, with the curved southbound line being laid on the right.

Metropole Layout

Above This scene from the past was photographed behind the Metropole on 10 April 1966, when the four surviving Standard cars were operating a Harrowside - Cabin service during a maintenance strike at Easter. Five of the last seven Standards - Nos. 40, 48, 49, 147 and 159 - survive in preservation, but these are the two that got away. No. 160 ran for just one more day before being withdrawn and scrapped, while 158 lasted until the end of the 1966 Illuminations, before going to Crich, where it was slowly dismembered for spare parts.

Centre The 1962 layout was unsatisfactory, with the southbound track veering suddenly into the path of oncoming vehicles, as demonstrated in July 1968 by twin-car 673/683, whose driver has prudently come to a halt. Cream Coronation 648 has tucked in behind.

Bottom In Spring 1969, the southbound line was straightened, and the centre track shortened. Balloon 718 passes the works, alongside the double shelter, in April.

Top Even without the awkward chicane by the hotel entrance, the unexpected confluence of trams and road traffic behind the Metropole was a perpetual problem. At least northbound trams tended to impose some sort of discipline, as here on 30 July 1978, with traffic dutifully following No. 700, while Brush car 622 tows a stricken Balloon back to depot.

Centre However the sudden appearance of a southbound tram round the Metropole corner could throw motorists into confusion. On 22 March 1981 works car 754, returning from a Sunday morning's rewiring, sends the driver of a Ford Capri onto the wrong side of the road.

Bottom In September 1993 a new layout was devised, with the southbound track on a painted tram lane. The general arrangement is seen here on 21 August 2010, with Standard 147 in the northbound lane.

Saturday Night Fever

Above Until the new road markings were introduced in 1993, traffic ran one-way (northwards) on Saturday and Sunday evenings during the Illuminations. In 1980 southbound Balloon 721 finds itself surrounded.

Below The following year, road traffic was kept to the east of the tracks by cones - a harbinger, perhaps, of today's Health & Safety culture, though there's not much sign of it amongst Dreadnought 59's passengers.

Stuck in the Snow

Above On 14 December 1981, coupled Balloons 722, 710 and 723 wait on the north corner of the Metropole.

Below The reason for the delay - a Hillman Avenger abandoned on the northbound track. The tram crews are formulating a plan of action, though the Council digger seems a rather drastic solution. In the end, they bounced the Avenger out of the way.

Oldest in the World

The northbound line behind the Metropole was - until 2010 - the world's oldest electric tram track in regular use. It was originally laid as a single-track conduit tramway in 1885. The road was widened, and a new southbound line was added in 1900, but the northbound track stayed in the same position until it was moved nearer the kerb at the end of the 2010 season.

Top The view from Dreadnought 59 on 3 June 1978, with Boat 605 ahead.

Centre Until the 1980s, parking was allowed on both sides of the road in winter. The driver of OMO car 2 - working a curtailed service between North Pier and Ash Street on 15 December 1981 - is weighing up his options. Eventually he just squeezed past.

Below Centenary car 641 heads south along the historic track on a misty 21 November 2005, 120 years and 19 days after the first conduit cars did the same.

The New Reservation

The Supertram project included a fairly radical solution to the age-old Metropole problem, though stopping short of diverting the line round the front of the hotel. During the winter of 2010/11 the track was rebuilt on reservation (nearer the west kerb) and road traffic had to make the best of what was left. Flexity 002 heads north on 19 September 2014.

The New Reservation

Above The rebuilt line opened on 6 May 2011, with trams running between Pleasure Beach and Cabin. Balloon 711 heads north on the first morning along virgin tracks with virgin paving.

Below The service was extended from Cabin to Little Bispham on 27 May. On 3 June Centenary 641 passed the ongoing road works, its tangerine livery celebrating Blackpool F.C.'s brief return to football's top flight.

The Changing Scene

Above In August 1968 a 1959 Austin A35 and a 1962 Wolseley 1500 run for cover as a 1953 Coronation bears down on them behind the Metropole. Not just any Coronation, but No. 652, one of the two rarest Blackpool trams of all - numerically speaking. Fleet numbers 649 and 652 were in use for only five months before the two Coronations (formerly 312 and 315) were withdrawn in October 1968.

Below Tram Only. Pantograph 167 - on loan from the National Tramway Museum - approaches North Pier on 26 May 2014.

The New Reservation

On 30 June 2011, Balloon 717 enjoys the luxury of the newly segregated track, just north of the Metropole.

Balloon 715 cruises past a queue of southbound traffic as it rounds the Metropole corner on 28 June 2011.

Onto the Street

Top The sight of a 17-ton Balloon looming in the path of northbound road traffic could be disconcerting for motorists. Balloon 726 on 12 June 2007.

Centre This taxi, passing OMO No. 9 in April 1980, looks set for a run up the North Promenade reservation. In April 1990 a night-time motorist drove more than a mile up the reservation before coming to an involuntary halt on the sleeper track at St Stephen's Avenue.

Below In 2007 bollards were erected at the start of the reservation. Driver-training Balloon 703 pauses there before venturing into the traffic on a misty 28 March 2007. 703 carried this 1980s colour scheme from 1999 until 2010, when it received Sunderland livery for its move to the Beamish museum.

7. North Promenade

The Promenade route was extended from the old conduit terminus at Cocker Street along North Promenade to the Gynn in May 1900 as a double track street tramway. In 1924 the tracks were transferred to a paved reservation on the site of the old footpath.

Above In the early evening of 30 July 1998, No. 707 (the first flat-fronted Balloon) stops at Cocker Street for a northbound passenger, four weeks after entering service.

Cocker Street

From 1885 to 1900, Cocker Street was the northern terminus of the tramway. Thereafter it was just another tram stop, and a fairly minor one at that, never having a shelter of any sort.

Above The general layout of the stops at Cocker Street - officially Cocker Square until 1990 - with Coronation 304 approaching the southbound stop on 31 October 2009. No. 304, the first of its class, was restored to original condition for the television programme *Salvage Squad* in 2002.

Centre The southbound stop was the normal constricted affair on the narrow footpath. Centenary car 648 - since restored as part of the heritage fleet - picks up a passenger on 8 December 2004.

Bottom Balloon 713's guard climbs back on board after helping a passenger off with a push-chair on 2 August 2008.

The track along North Promenade was completely rebuilt during the winter of 2010/11. When the line reopened on 6 May, the tram stops at Cocker Street were reinstated, but only for one season. The northbound stop was this undistinguished dustbin, just south of the old stop. Balloon 715 passes on 4 July 2011.

Cocker Street disappeared from the tramway itinerary at the end of the 2011 season. Flexity 014 sails past the site of the old northbound stop on 25 June 2013.

Pleasant Street

Above The next stop after Cocker Street - and today the first stop after North Pier - was Pleasant Street, also sometimes known as *Carlton Hotel*. On 18 February 1961, Bispham Depot's Brush car 301 approaches Pleasant Street *en route* to Central Station, as the Tower was then known on the trams. It wasn't a common destination for southbound cars at the time. In the background is the cast-iron shelter at the Imperial Hotel.

Centre Railcoach 224 reverses over the Carlton crossover during single-line working in January 1962. At one time there were four crossovers on North Promenade, but by 1962 there was just this one, which was removed in December 1975. Now there are none between North Pier and Cabin.

Bottom No. 224 sets off wrong-line for North Pier and then Starr Gate. It was fairly unusual that winter to see a railcoach on the Starr Gate - Fleetwood service, which was normally operated by Coronations. However No. 224 was the latest railcoach to be overhauled, having been turned out in September 1961 with a fixed (instead of sliding) roof.

Above In January 1962, Coronation 322 passes Pleasant Street's cast-iron shelter - one of the oldest on the Promenade, dating from 1912 - before crossing over to regain the northbound track.

Right Late in 1971, the adjacent stops at the Imperial Hotel and Pleasant Street received the first Adshels on the tramway. Adshel (formed in 1969 by two advertising agencies) had already supplied Blackpool with 17 free bus shelters in return for advertising rights. Pleasant Street was the town's 19th Adshel, hence the number 0019 (the stop names were added in 1980). Centenary 641 pulls away from the shelter in May 1988. (*Alan Spencer*)

Below The Adshel in turn was replaced in 1996 by a green and cream Abacus shelter, which was nearing the end of its career on 4 October 2010. As was Centenary car 647, pulling up at the southbound stop.

Pleasant Street

Above On 9 August 2007 a spot of repaving is interrupted by the arrival of Standard car 147.

Centre Balloon 703 passes Pleasant Street on 7 June 2010 during a farewell run before leaving for Beamish Museum. Sunderland Corporation - whose livery 703 bears - had cars of similar design.

Bottom The stop at Pleasant Street was closed throughout the 2011 season while the Supertram platforms were built. By the time Balloon 711 passed through the stop on 4 July, a new Trueform shelter had replaced the Abacus. Most of the platforms from here northwards are surfaced in utilitarian tarmac, rather than the classier paving used further south. The proliferation of safety barriers - a feature of the Supertram project - seemed to create as many hazards as it prevented.

Top Time was when ailing trams being towed back to depot were a common sight, but much less so these days. Flexity 014 pulls 015 past the Carlton Hotel on 17 July 2013.

Bottom Low-floor access has transformed the tramway for those with wheel-chairs and push-chairs. Early-morning passengers prepare to board Flexity 005 at Pleasant Street on 12 June 2014. As with the old tramway, the narrow pavement means that North Promenade has shelters only on the northbound track.

Imperial Hotel

After Pleasant Street came the Imperial Hotel stop, also known in the past as *Park House* (from the hotel next door) and sometimes *Redmans* (who owned it). The Imperial opened in June 1867. Charles Dickens stayed for two nights in April 1869 during his last nationwide reading tour, which ended prematurely at Preston because of the writer's health.

Above The Donald McGill theme for the 1981 Illuminations looks rather out of place in front of Blackpool's premier hotel. OMO car 3 departs for Fleetwood; the rear blind on one-man cars was left blank to save the driver having to leave his post (and cash) to change it.

Centre The view from the open balcony of Standard car 40 approaching the southbound stop at the Imperial in 1961, as a Promenade Circular passes the cast-iron shelter.

Bottom The same view in 1983, complete with Adshel and Balloon 722, wearing the unique green V which it carried from May to August that summer. (*Alan Spencer collection*)

True Blue

Above The Imperial was the Conservative Party's traditional headquarters during their annual conference. In 2007 they commissioned this special livery on Balloon 713, which ran between Little Bispham and Pleasure Beach during the conference to serve the main hotels, here passing the speed camera outside the high-security Imperial on 1 October. In the background is Wilton Parade tram stop.

On 4 October 2009, blue Balloon 718 passes the Abacus shelter which replaced the Adshel, and draws up at the southbound stop.

Imperial Hotel

Above (left) The Imperial tram stop - like that at Cocker Street - survived the reconstruction of the North Promenade tramway in 2010/11, but only for one season while the adjacent stops at Pleasant Street and Wilton Parade were rebuilt with Supertram platforms. As at Cocker Street, the Imperial was served during 2011 by this temporary stop sign in a barrel. Boat 600 draws up at the Imperial on 3 July 2011, with the site of the former shelter visible just beyond.

Above (right) All that remains of the Imperial stop today is this feeder box on the footpath, labelled *Tram Shelter Supply.* Flexity 004 speeds past regardless on 1 July 2014.

Driver-training Flexity 006, running wrong-line to Starr Gate depot, passes the Imperial on 7 March 2012, with No. 001 following at Wilton Parade. Drivers these days are instructed to keep well behind the car in front. As a result, queues of trams - and hopefully rear-end collisions - are largely a thing of the past.

Wilton Parade

Wilton Parade is the side street at the northern end of the Imperial Hotel, and has the usual crescent and curving path leading down to the Middle Walk. Initially the tram stop took its name from the terrace just to the north - Rutland Gate.

Above Balloon 242 leaves Wilton Parade for Starr Gate in August 1961. The cast-iron shelter dates from 1925.

Centre The southbound track between the Imperial Hotel and Gynn Square was relaid during the winter of 1976/77. Brush car 625 deputises for 624, the normal incumbent, as Permanent Way car, just south of Wilton Parade. (*Fylde Tramway Society archive*)

Bottom In 1972 the cast-iron shelter was replaced by the usual Adshel. OMO car 6 is passing on 3 June 1978, with a southbound OMO approaching the Imperial stop.

Wilton Parade

Abacus Comes, Abacus Goes

Above Fleetwood Box car 40, having climbed the slope from Warley Road, passes Wilton Parade's new Abacus shelter on 24 May 2000. No. 40 was built in 1914 (to an 1898 design) and after withdrawal in 1936 served as a works car until being restored for the 75th Anniversary in 1960.

Left The remains of the Abacus on 29 April 2011 during construction of the Supertram stop.

Wilton Parade stop was closed throughout 2011 while the Supertram platforms were built. Centenary 648 passes the work site on 29 May.

Wilton Parade

Above Balloon 717 on heritage duty - with heritage destination - passes Wilton Parade's Supertram stop and the Imperial Hotel on 25 August 2012.

Below Flexity 012 draws up at Wilton Parade's northbound platform on 9 June 2014.

Derby Road

Above Derby Road - the next stop after Wilton Parade - was the first to have one of Blackpool's iconic cast-iron shelters, erected in 1911 and made by David Rowell of Westminster. The land on the right, between Derby Road and Warley Road, was known as the Pembroke Estate, and in 1933 was earmarked for a 1,780-bedroom hotel. Instead the Corporation bought it in 1935 for £55,000 and built the Derby Baths - the second largest in the country after those at Wembley. The baths opened in July 1939, and are directly behind Coronation 324 leaving Derby Road stop in 1961.

Below Standard car 160 approaches Derby Road from Wilton Parade in August 1961.

Derby Road

The stop and shelter were originally opposite Derby Road but were moved northwards when the reservation was built in 1924.

Above An English Electric railcoach leaves Derby Road stop in 1961. Apart from the baths, the rest of the Pembroke Estate remained undeveloped for forty years.

Centre The view from a Promenade Circular Boat as it approaches Derby Road shelter on 24 July 1969. (*Clyde L. Shoebridge*)

Bottom Derby Road stop closed in 1969/70, so never had an Adshel. Brush car 626 passes the site in 1971, by which time the block on the corner of Derby Road had been demolished in preparation for the erection of the Pembroke Hotel in 1977. The hotel didn't open until 1982. It became the Stakis in 1997 and the Hilton in 2000.

Warley Road

The final crescent - and tram stop - on North Promenade was at Warley Road. This was one of the first stops to have a cast-iron shelter, built in 1912 by Walter MacFarlane of Glasgow, to a design very similar to the nearby Rowell shelter at Derby Road.

Above Coronation 318, approaching Warley Road shelter, passes Derby Baths on 18 February 1961. Blackpool's tram shelters were usually green with cream windows, but many were painted cream for Coronation year in 1953.

Centre By 1968 the shelter - or rather the footpath - was showing signs of subsidence. Coronation 650 (another fleeting fleet number, lasting only two seasons) stops to pick up passengers in the summer of 1968. Balloons 706 and 711 pass each other on a supplementary Starr Gate - Bispham service.

Bottom Balloon 710 approaches the leaning shelter on 24 July 1969. (*Clyde L. Shoebridge*)

Warley Road

Top Warley Road received the statutory Adshel in 1972. Balloon 719 drops off passengers on 16 September 1979. The shelter is now level, if not the pavement.

Centre A three-car battering-ram roars past Warley Road, as cars 722, 710 and 723 clear the track on 14 December 1981. Warley Road stop was in a dip; following a steady descent from Pleasant Street, the tracks rose again before reaching the Gynn curve.

Below When the Adshels were given names in 1980, Warley Road became *Derby Baths*, but by the end of May 1990, the name had been painted out, as demolition of the baths was under way - an unpopular process, judging by the graffiti. Boat 605 had just been restored to original 1934 livery.

Warley Road

Top Warley Road's Adshel was removed in 1996 and replaced by an Abacus. Liverpool 762 passes on 16 September 2010.

Bottom The relaid track, with Centenary car 648 passing Warley Road on 9 May 2011. The shelter was out of use, though it re-opened later in the summer, only for the stop to close permanently at the end of the season.

North from Warley Road

Above Balloon 717 leaves Warley Road on 20 August 2012. When the tram tracks were moved from the street onto the pavement in 1924, a new footpath was cantilevered out over the Middle Walk.

Centre The same tram in the same place (with the Hilton Hotel in the background) but this is the lower-deck of the newly restored 717 on 23 August 2008.

Bottom Another newly restored tram turns onto North Promenade from the Gynn and heads for Warley Road in August 1960. Fleetwood Rack 2 was returned to service for the 75th Anniversary in 1960, and donated to the National Tramway Museum three years later. It revisited Blackpool briefly in 1998 and 2010.

Round to the Gynn

Top OMO car 8 heads round the curve from North Promenade towards the Gynn on 1 November 2010.

Bottom Flexity 015 flexes round the curve on 16 May 2014.

8. The Gynn

The track from the Gynn up to the Cliffs Hotel (the borough boundary at the time) was built in 1898 by Blackpool Corporation as part of the Fleetwood Tramroad Company's route from Talbot Road Station to Fleetwood. Even after comprehensive rebuilding, its layout remains something of a hybrid - paved like the Corporation's Promenade route, but with Tramroad-style centre poles.

Above Flexity 003 pulls away up the hill from the northbound Supertram platform on 25 June 2013.

A Quick Look Back

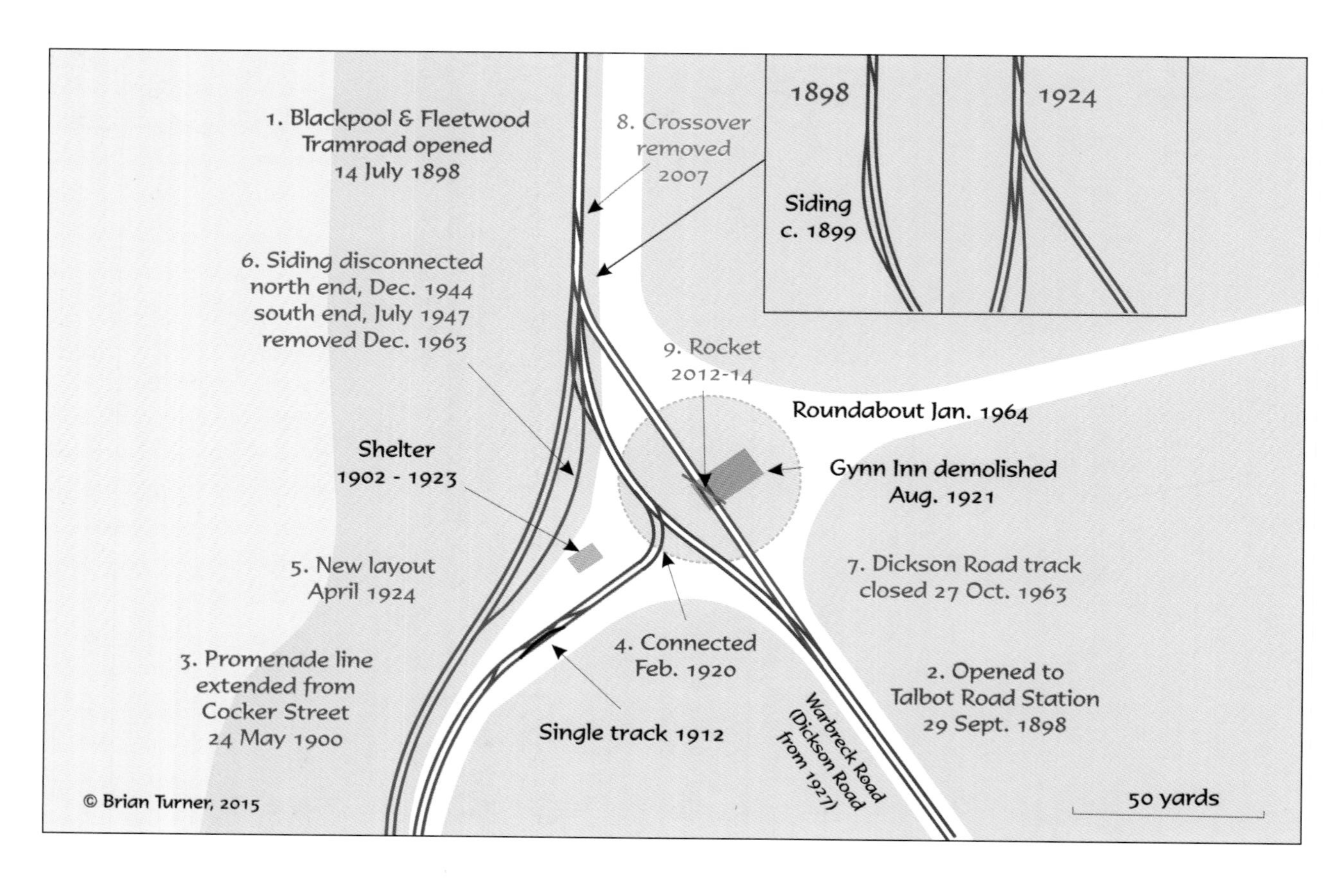

Above This series isn't normally concerned with the period before 1960, but it's perhaps worth making an exception at the Gynn, where today's bland layout - lacking even a crossover - gives scant indication of the place's importance in the story of Blackpool's tramways. The map above shows the key developments.

Below The Gynn in 1907, with Dreadnought 22 at the Promenade terminus and Yank 34 on the Tramroad leading up to Uncle Tom's Cabin, where (for a few months) the line passed between old and new versions of the building.

Author's note *This picture has much to answer for. I first came across it in a family postcard album at the age of seven, when my experience of trams was limited to the stately Bury bogie cars which took me to school. Dreadnought 22, with its ungrammatical advertisement, made a lasting impression - the start of a lifelong interest in the Blackpool tramway and its history.*

The Gynn Curve

Above Coronation 323 rounds the elegant reverse curve from North Promenade on 18 February 1961.

Centre On 2 July 1960, Standard car 41 arrives at the northbound Promenade shelter (1924). On the right is the southbound steel shelter (1945) and the remains of the little-used siding laid in 1924 for the Fleetwood - Gynn turnbacks. No. 41 was withdrawn three weeks later after an accident.

Bottom Pantograph No. 170 heads down the main line on its way to Pleasure Beach for the 75th Anniversary procession on 29 September 1960. 170's guard is attending to the first fare-paying passengers to ride along the Promenade on a Pantograph car for many years.

Gynn Junction

Top An English Electric railcoach turns off across Gynn Square to North Station around 1955, with the northbound shelter (1931) for cars coming from Dickson Road on the left, though without a stop sign. (*Jim Copland, Malcolm King collection*)

Centre The automatic points at the Gynn were a regular source of trouble. In 1961 new twin-car 281/T1 and railcoach 217 wait while Karrier tower wagon 238 of 1948 carries out repairs. The unloading stop was for North Station cars only.

Below From 1928 to 1960 the Pantograph cars were fixtures on the North Station route, turning off the Promenade at the Gynn. For the second half of their careers they appeared only in the season. No. 170 heads south across Gynn Square during an enthusiasts' tour on 4 June 1961, two months after the Pantographs made their last brief appearance in service at Easter.

Gynn Crossover

The crossover at the Gynn dated back to the opening of the Fleetwood Tramroad in July 1898, and served as the southern terminus of the line for its first ten weeks.

Above In May 1961 a Brush car (one of four trams supplied by Bispham Depot for the Starr Gate - Fleetwood service) passes the crossover and some classic permanent-way paraphernalia.

Centre Gynn turnbacks were relatively rare after the three-track layout at Cabin opened in May 1944. However at Easter 1966, newly painted 253 is about to reverse. From the state of the grooves, 253 isn't the first to use the crossover that day, though not enough to shine the rails.

Bottom The most common use of the crossover was during single-line working. On 2 February 1980 the inspector hands the single-line staff to the driver of northbound OMO 6 (reversing to use the east track as far as Cabin) before retreating to withdrawn PD/3 No. 377.

Northbound Stops

Above The seaward side of the No. 1 shelter, seen from the sunken gardens on 2 July 1960 - the first day of Standard car operation that season - with No. 48 running down the hill from the Cliffs Hotel.

Jubilee 761 calls at the Gynn in October 1980. 761's blind-maker found *Ash Street, Fleetwood* - not to mention *Tour of Illuminations* - quite a challenge. The second Jubilee, No. 762, had a slightly taller aperture with space for two lines.

The Gynn in the bleak mid-winter. A lone sea angler climbs aboard OMO 6 on 2 February 1980.

Ten days after entering service, Centenary car 643 stands at the Adshel on 28 February 1987, with Jubilee 762 approaching.

Northbound Stop

Above In 1996 the Adshel gave way to an Abacus, sited several yards further north - one of several stops which developed a curious northward drift in recent years. Here the Abacus itself is almost at the end of its life on 25 September 2010, as Marton Box car 31 pulls away from the stop, and Standard 147 leans into the curve. No. 31 had no roller blind - hence the destination.

Centre The Abacus was mainly clad in solid panels, suitably painted green and cream. Manchester 765 passes on 28 September 2010.

Bottom For the 2011 season the Abacus has gone, leaving only this new style of stop sign. Balloon 720 drops off passengers via its fancy new doors on 14 July, its first day in passenger service after a five-year absence. Something of a false dawn, as 720 made only spasmodic appearances during the rest of 2011 and none at all in the next three years.

Southbound Stop

Top Coronations 309 and 314 pass at the Gynn on 14 May 1966 between the cast-iron northbound shelter and the steel southbound shelter - still in its original state, with the queue facing south.

Centre Twenty years later, in July 1986, car 10 from the Hill of Howth tramway (near Dublin) approaches the stop. The direction of the shelter was reversed in 1972. No. 10 had just been restored for its owners, the National Tramway Museum; it ran at Blackpool from September 1985 to October 1989.

Below The sub-station on the left was part of the rebuilding of the electrical and overhead system in 1995/96. The wartime steel shelter - having clocked up a praiseworthy 53 years - was back in green and cream when Balloon 723 called on 17 August 1998, but was demolished in the following March.

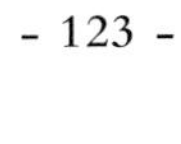

Southbound Stop

Top The steel shelter was followed in June 1999 by the usual two-bay Abacus, seen here on 27 July that year. Centenary car 642 is manfully towing twin-car 684/674 back to Rigby Road, using the momentum from the downhill run to surmount the climb up to North Promenade.

Centre The far bay of the Abacus was given a leg-up in 2000/01 (perhaps someone banged their head). Jubilee 762, seen at the shelter on 23 September 2009, was named *Stuart L. Pillar* after its designer, in 2008.

Below The Abacus disappeared when the track was relaid in 2010/11, and for the next season the stop was marked by one of the short-lived 2011-style signs, but no shelter. Balloon 717 calls on 13 July.

The Roadliner

The Roadliner articulated tram, designed by Professor Lewis Lesley of Liverpool University, was tested on and off at Blackpool from 1998. During the winter of 2006/07 it underwent trials between Cleveleys and the Gynn, while the regular tram service was running only between Thornton Gate and Fleetwood.

Above The Roadliner crosses over at the Gynn on 22 January 2007. Two days later, the experiment came to a premature end when the car caught fire at Foxhall whilst returning to Rigby Road.

Centre A passenger's view at the Gynn on 1 December 2006. Not that the car ever carried passengers at Blackpool, though it did at Birkenhead in 2005.

Below (left) The fully-fitted interior incorporated a *Next Stop* display.

Below (right) The cab was rather less sophisticated.

Above On a threatening 25 May 2014, restored twin-car 272/T2 passes the Gynn, while the illuminated Rocket looks set to head up Dickson Road, as it did for 32 years in its previous guise as Pantograph car 168.

Centre Much like this - the same angle on 2 July 1960.

Bottom The Rocket was displayed from August 2012 to June 2014 in the centre of the roundabout, on the site of the original Gynn Inn (*see map on page 116*).

Opposite (top) The Supertram platforms - like all their ilk - were built on straight track, and hence had to be further up the hill than the old stops. Northbound 012 passes 016 on 19 September 2012.

Opposite (bottom) Approaching the southbound stop on 28 April 2014, No. 003 passes the Savoy Hotel (far right). Across King George Avenue is the Grade II listed Savoy Garage - still with its original turntable and vehicle lift. Hotel and garage were built in 1915 to the design of Tom G. Lumb, who built the Fleetwood Tramroad.

WoWtels
.com
Starr Gate

Weddings & Celebrations
003

Up to the Cliffs

Top A Pantograph car climbs the gradient from the Gynn in July 1960, with the Cliffs Hotel on the crest of the hill. The hotel's unified appearance is deceptive. Like Topsy in (appropriately) *Uncle Tom's Cabin,* the Cliffs Hotel 'just growed'. The south elevation (on King Edward Avenue) opened in 1921 as a small private hotel called the Bryn Tivy. In the mid-1920s it was extended slightly northwards, and renamed the Cliffs, but the rest of the hotel wasn't built until 1937, more than doubling its size.

Centre On 23 July 1960, Fleetwood Rack No. 2 - newly restored for the 75th Anniversary - heads north from the Cliffs Hotel towards Uncle Tom's Cabin, where two Standard cars are reversing. The centre poles on the hybrid section between Gynn and Cabin are cream, Promenade style. A few years earlier they were green, Tramroad style *(see page 118)*.

Below In July 1971, Balloon 717 leaves the Cliffs Hotel, with 713 approaching from Uncle Tom's Cabin. This stretch - originally sleeper track - was paved in 1924 when the Corporation (having taken over the Tramroad in 1920) extended the Promenade route to the Cabin.

Cliffs Hotel

Above Despite its exposed location, the Cliffs Hotel stop didn't have a tram shelter until 1996, when suddenly it got two. The new Abacus shelters are seen on 6 July 1997 with Balloon 713.

Centre Balloon 702 at the northbound shelter on 7 July 2005. 702 carried 1970s livery from September 2004 until May 2010, when it departed for preservation at Heaton Park.

Bottom The Abacus shelters disappeared after the 2010 season, and during the next year the Supertram platforms were built on the same site. For the 2011 season the stops had to be moved slightly southwards. Just before the line reopened, the displaced signs from Wilton Parade (which was closed throughout 2011) were placed at the Cliffs. Centenary 644 passes during test running on 5 May. By the following day, when tram service to the Cabin resumed, the stops had received new 2011-style signs. (*James Millington*)

Cliffs Hotel

Above Balloon 719 returned to service with its new widened entrance during half-term week, 2012. Here it passes 709 at the Cliffs Hotel on 2 November.

Below Flexity 013 approaches the northbound shelter (under repair) on 25 June 2013. In view of the reduction in stops elsewhere on the Promenade, and the proximity of those at Gynn and the Cabin, it's surprising that the Cliffs Hotel survived as a Supertram stop.

9. Uncle Tom's Cabin

Uncle Tom's Cabin began life in the 1850s as a small hut on the cliff-top selling sweets, and grew into a vaguely disreputable entertainment complex before falling into the sea in 1907. It was replaced by the public house which still stands on the east side of the road. From 1898 until the Corporation took over in 1920, the Cabin was served by the Fleetwood Tramroad. A third track was laid in May 1944.

Above Balloon 700 leaves the Cabin for Fleetwood on 14 April 2007. On the right is the Castle (*see page 143*).

Indian Summer of the Standards

On 6 August 1960, the seven surviving Standard cars (Nos. 40, 48, 49, 147 and 158-160) were working Promenade specials as far as the Cabin.

Top Car 49 waits on the centre line, with a Boat and two railcoaches on the sleeper track.

Centre No. 49 sets off behind a southbound Pantograph car, passing the arriving 160 (and the photographer's transport, leaning against a traction pole).

Below No. 160 then takes the centre track, as Dreadnought 59 (decorated for Daily Mirror Week) passes, followed by a Pantograph and a Coronation - quite a display. On the left is the tram station and lift to the Promenade.

Paddleboat at Uncle Tom's

In a fitting American combination, the Mississippi paddleboat *Blackpool Belle* spent an hour at Uncle Tom's Cabin on 6 July 1966, along with the Bluebell Girls from Paris, filming a trailer for Ken Dodd's television series.

Above Ken Dodd receives a crash course on the ticket machine from General Manager Joseph Franklin. On the platform of the *Belle,* Chief Engineer Alan Williams is more concerned with the Bluebell Girls, holding their stomachs in as twin-car 274/T4 squeezes past.

Right Ready to start filming. The Blackpool Belle was built in 1959 on the remains of toastrack No. 163.

Turning at the Cabin

The virtually unbroken sequence of seafront hotels - extending all the way from the Metropole - came to an end at the Cabin, making the three-track layout there a natural location to turn trams back in the season.

Left The inspector gives 710's driver his instructions while he changes the blind before reversing on 10 August 1997.

Below 602's guard resets the points as the Boat car runs onto the centre track on 6 May 2006. Centenary car 641 approaches from St Stephen's Avenue.

Opposite (top) Turning 600's trolley on 25 July 2006 in a temperature of 88°F. Blackpool's record temperature of 91°F was equalled during the previous week. Balloon 719, the Walls Ice Cream tram (on the left) would have done good business had it still been fitted with an ice-cream counter, as it was during 1996 (*inset*).

Opposite (bottom) Twin-car 672/682 leaves the centre track on 11 July 1999 and approaches the southbound stop, temporarily without a shelter (*see page 141*).

FYLDE TRAMWAY SOCIETY
FTS
CABIN
600
Wall's

TWIN CAR
PLEASURE BEACH
672
Shops
Coins
Tram Stop
Southbound

Back to Two Tracks

During the winter of 2007/08 the track at Cabin was completely relaid, removing the third track after 63 years, and relocating the crossover further north to allow space for the Supertram platforms. When services restarted on 21 March, trams initially ran only between Starr Gate and Cabin.

Above The Abacus shelter remained in use at the northbound stop. Centenaries 643 and 646 turn at the Cabin on 28 March 2008.

Centre On the same day, Balloon 723 prepares to turn on the new crossover, which was so far north that cars had to run onto the sleeper track to reverse.

Bottom This proved tricky with heritage cars, and two strips of tarmac were soon laid for the benefit of guards turning the trolley. Driver-training Balloon 701 passes on 6 May 2008.

Top Supertram platforms began to appear at the Cabin in 2010. Fleetwood Box car 40 passes the new northbound platform and old shelter on 25 September.

Bottom After another winter closure, trams returned to the Cabin - but no further - on 6 May 2011. Jubilee car 761 reverses three days later.

Northbound Stop

Above Ever since 1903, northbound passengers at the Cabin had enjoyed the protection of a tram station. In 1930 when J.C. Robinson, the Borough Architect, designed a lift to take visitors down to the lower promenade, the building incorporated a new station, seen here in February 1979, doubling up as a radio tower, this being the highest point on the coast for many miles, at 90 feet above sea level. Balloons 716 and 703 enjoy a rare winter outing.

Below In this exposed spot, passengers still had to brave the weather to board the trams. Jubilee 762 picks up on 14 January 1985.

Northbound Stop

Top When the Cabin lift was reconstructed between 1988 and 1990, Robinson's classical tram station was replaced by a prosaic Adshel. On 29 March 1994 the shelter is made to look rather grander than it really was by the roof of the public toilets behind. Balloon 721 reverses while withdrawn OMO 11 - now distinctly down at heel - drags itself to Fleetwood on a test run for the Roadliner project.

Centre The 1988 Adshel eventually went the way of all Adshels - removed overnight in 1996 after a dispute with Blackpool Council over maintenance - and was replaced by this more stylish two-bay Abacus. Balloon 711, very briefly wearing an all-yellow livery, unloads on 13 August 2007.

Below Car 147 at the Abacus on 1 May 2005, showing the truncated Cabin lift - now Grade II listed, even without Robinson's tram station.

Southbound Stops

Above Since the 1940s there had been two southbound steel shelters at the Cabin - one for North Station and the other for Promenade and Squire's Gate cars. Standard car 48 pulls up at the Promenade shelter in August 1961.

Below The North Station shelter was near the points, and after the Dickson Road route closed in 1963, it became the Promenade shelter, and the other one was removed. In this timeless scene, 147 and 160 meet by the shelter while working a service between Cabin and Harrowside at Easter 1966.

Southbound Stop

Above In 1972 the wartime steel shelter was replaced - like those at the Tower and North Pier - by a wooden structure made at Rigby Road. In April 1980, Jubilee 761 is followed by OMO 10, Brush cars 621 and 626 and OMO 6, as they wait for a problem to be sorted out. On the left is new Bedford tower wagon 439.

Centre In the Spring of 1999 the wooden shelter was removed, leaving the southbound stop devoid for a while. Twin-car 684/674 draws up at the unsheltered stop on 18 June 1999.

Bottom Eventually a replacement Abacus appeared, though it was only a single bay long (presumably because of the assorted safety barriers which had sprung up around the stop). Jubilee 762 is loading on 23 October 2007.

Shelters Galore

The Supertram platforms and shelters were completed early in 2011, and during that summer there were four tram shelters at Cabin, though only one was in use. Balloon 632 - restored to 1970s condition - demonstrates.

Above Three of the shelters are visible on 4 November 2011, as 632 heads up to the new crossover to reverse, passing the northbound Abacus - now out of use and obstructed by the Supertram platform with its Trueform Elite shelter. On the right is the southbound Supertram shelter.

Centre The fourth shelter - the southbound Abacus - remains in use, with 632 leading Balloon 717 on 29 May 2011.

Bottom Despite the plethora of shelters in 2011, northbound passengers had to manage without. Instead they used a one-season stop (with 2011-style sign) just south of the Supertram platforms. It is seen here with 632, 717 and 754 on 29 May.

Above Not the most romantic spot to sunbathe. There was rather more romance attached to the building on the other side of the line. It was built in 1907 after the style of a chateau by a Blackpool solicitor for his new French bride. She preferred to live in France, and the Castle - as it was always known - remained empty for over 30 years before becoming a nightclub in September 1939. It has been a casino for many years. Flexity 005 heads north on 30 June 2014.

Below Widened Balloon 700 leaves the northbound platform on 29 July 2012.

Heritage Stops

The Cabin heritage stops are well south of the Supertram platforms, and nearly halfway to the Cliffs Hotel. Balloon 717 waits on 16 August 2012.

Restored twin-car 272/T2 is heading for a downpour as it passes the Supertram platform and approaches the heritage stop on 25 May 2014, with the second (1907) Uncle Tom's Cabin on the left.

10. Along the Cliffs

Leaving Uncle Tom's Cabin, the tramway runs - almost straight and level - along the cliff-tops to Cavendish Road, the last stop before Bispham. In Tramroad Company days there were no stops at all along this stretch, and the only buildings were a cottage on the sea side of the line near Miners' Home, and Bank Farm at the present St Stephen's Avenue.

Above Restored OMO car No. 8 passes Lowther Avenue stop on 1 November 2010.

St Stephen's Avenue

Above Three coupled Balloons - from front to rear, Nos. 722, 710 and 723 - race down the hill from the Cabin towards St Stephen's Avenue, to clear the Tramroad on 14 December 1981.

Centre No. 722 on its own at the same spot on 23 August 1980. During the 1970s the deteriorating concrete fencing was crudely patched with old angle-iron which had served - not very effectively - as check-rail on the Tramroad. The fencing on the landward side was usually more presentable. (*Alan Spencer collection*)

Bottom The stop at St Stephen's was opened in 1926 and had a shelter from the start. There wasn't room on the footpath for the usual oval cast-iron shelter, so the foundry at Rigby Road concocted a rectangular version, using some of the same castings. It is seen here looking rather sorry for itself in June 1984, a few weeks before it disappeared. In the background OMO car 5 heads north.

St Stephen's Avenue

In August 1984 the cast-iron shelter was replaced by a distinctive new design, with the Blackpool crest etched on smoked glass.

Above On 1 May 1997 Brush car 621 loads at the crested shelter.

Right The etched crest is seen here on an identical shelter erected at Revoe Gymnasium to replace an oval cast-iron shelter which once served the Central Drive tramway. These seem to have been the only two examples.

Below The flagman in the top picture was part of the permanent way gang. Centenary 645 passes, on the same May Day 1997.

St Stephen's Avenue

Above The crested shelter gave way to the standard Abacus design in 1999. Standard car 147 passes on 22 July 2006. The traction poles - originally red and cream in 1996 - were painted grey in the Spring of 2005.

Centre Serious stuff. Colas Rail (the contractors who relaid the Tramroad between Gynn and Norbreck in 2007/08) brought this main-line Plasser & Theurer tamper by road to Bispham tram station. On 19 March 2008 it is approaching St Stephen's Avenue.

Bottom When the track was relaid, the paving at St Stephen's was replaced by tarmac. Coronation 660 passes on 29 September 2010. The stop closed with the old tramway in November 2011.

The Changing Tramroad

Above The Tramroad in 1978, with OMO car 6 approaching St Stephen's Avenue on 3 June. The 1930s-style concrete fencing is largely intact, with just the odd length of angle-iron, which also remains in use as check-rail.

Below The same scene - slightly further south - thirty years on, with Brush car 631 on 1 July 2008. Completely new (flat-bottomed) track, fencing and overhead since 1978, though the greensward along the cliffs is not what it used to be.

Lowther Avenue

Top Lowther Avenue stop dates from 1930, and in August 1968 was still redolent of the Tramroad in the Thirties - concrete fencing, sprung gates, wooden name-board, central lamp standard and 1936-style cast-iron shelter. No. 663 meets the last cream Coronation, No. 648, which was withdrawn a few weeks later.

Bottom Looking the other way on 4 December 1965, Coronation 314 approaches Lowther Avenue.

Lowther Avenue

A distinctive feature of Lowther Avenue stop - and a good vantage point for photographers - is the sub-station which fed the Illuminations tableaux along the cliffs.

Above OMO car 9 leaves the stop on 13 January 1979. Part of the 1930s-style concrete fencing by the sub-station was still there in 2014 (*see page 156*).

Centre Seen from the sub-station on 21 April 1979, a cheerful party takes a last ride on the *Blackpool Belle* before its departure for America. The TT (Trailer Tram) sign is a marker for twin-car drivers. (*Fylde Tramway Society archive*)

Bottom Centenary car 641 calls on 8 July 1984, two days after entering service. The cast-iron shelter had been renovated in 1975, though hardly improved, being painted an unappealing mustard shade and losing most of its windows in favour of Darvic plastic.

End of the Cast-iron Shelter

The cast-iron shelter was removed without replacement in the summer of 2005, having at least enjoyed the dignity of green and cream since 1991. Most of the windows have been replaced, though not the original art-deco Flemish-glass quarter-lights.

Top Balloon 710 in Metro Coastlines Line 7 livery on 17 September 2004.

Centre The stop with shelter and name-board - of sorts - on 1 March 2005.

Below Twin-car 672/682 approaches the northbound stop on 12 May 2005. After the twin-cars were withdrawn in 2011, 672/682 was added to the heritage fleet, and returned to its original cream livery as 272/T2 (*see page 39*).

Lowther Avenue

Construction of Lowther Avenue's Supertram stops began in 2010. On 16 September, Liverpool 762 passes the new northbound platform.

The Western Train southbound with a school party on 29 June 2011.

Lowther Avenue

Brush car 632 leaves the old stop on 30 September 2011.

Balloon 720 on 14 July 2011, its first day in service with widened entrance.

Last-minute Changes

Top Driver-training Flexity 002 passes Lowther Avenue on 7 February 2012, with the Supertram stop apparently ready for opening, with platforms, shelters, lamps and name-board, though the lighting turned out to be non-functional.

Centre Rather at the eleventh hour, it was decided - at the Rail Regulator's edict, apparently, after an accident on another system - that all stops on the sleeper track should be paved. On 14 March 2012, sheets of a resin-based material are being laid between the running rails. Amidst all this high technology, traditionalists (or at least the author) took comfort from the use of classic wooden cattle-guards, which might have come straight from the Fleetwood Tramroad.

Below Paved from platform to platform, Lowther Avenue opened for Supertram business on 4 April 2012. Two days later a weekend heritage service started, but - because of the gap between tram and platform - couldn't use the new stops, to the disappointment of these passengers anticipating an open-air ride on 26 May.

New Paving

Top With characteristic Blackpool inconsistency, some stops had wall-to-wall resin, while others had paving only between the running rails. Lowther Avenue started with the former, but finished with the latter, as seen here on 15 April 2014, with Flexity 004.

Centre High-tech track maintenance at Lowther Avenue on 21 May 2014, using a Geismar trolley to measure gauge and rail levels. On the cliffs, PW bus 1054 (ex-Metrorider 512) stands by the abandoned Hire-a-Bike station, waiting to follow the Geismar towards Uncle Tom's Cabin. The tracks have just been resurfaced with rubber panels (*see page 163*).

Flexity 003 arrives on 14 May, with the rubber paving almost complete. Near the sub-station is one of the few surviving fragments of 1930s concrete fencing.

Miners' Home

Miners' Home tram stop dated from June 1927, when the Lancashire & Cheshire Miners' Convalescent Home was officially opened by the Prince of Wales. The building was funded by a levy of 1d. per ton on all coal mined in the two counties.

Above The imposing convalescent home - Grade II listed since 1995 - is seen in July 1980, with Balloon 723. The seaward fencing is mainly old check-rail. (*Fylde Tramway Society archive*)

Centre Miners' Home stop was unusual in being on an embankment. Until 1907 there was a cottage in the hollow on the seaward side of the line here. A northbound Coronation calls on 1 January 1962. In front of the convalescent home can be seen the unusual rectangular cast-iron shelter (*see next page*).

Bottom The filling material for the embankment presumably came from the cutting between Miners' Home and Lowther Avenue when the line was built in 1897. An English Electric railcoach on the North Station route leaves Miners' Home on 1 January 1962.

Miners' Home

Above Balloon 707 passes Dreadnought 59 at the Miners' Home on 3 June 1978.

Centre Although the Home's official opening was in 1927, the first patients didn't arrive until March 1931. For their benefit a rectangular cast-iron shelter was built in 1930. It was similar to the one erected at St Stephen's Avenue in 1926 (*see page 146*) though the arrangement of the panels was different. It is seen here in June 1984.

Bottom Originally the shelter was mainly glass. An official examination in January 1970 revealed '24 plain glass windows broken, 10 leaded plain glass windows broken. 20 plain glass windows discoloured' and recommended 'full replacement (92 windows) with Darvic, leaving one window plain glass at both ends, to view trams.' This was the grim result. The shelter survived until August 1988, when it was replaced by an Adshel. Although Adshels were standard along the Promenade, they were rare on the Tramroad, and this was the only one between Cabin and Anchorsholme Lane. Despite - or because of - this, the shelter seems to have evaded the camera during its eight-year existence.

Miners' Home

Top Brush car 637 - newly painted in 1980s-style with green band - loads at the cast-iron shelter on 2 April 1984.

Centre Banished. Sheffield 513 leaves Miners' Home stop in disgrace on 19 May 2003. The previous afternoon, 513 had derailed so comprehensively on the northbound track near St Stephen's Avenue that it was left there all night. After re-railing next morning, 513 is being towed back to Rigby Road by Balloon 720. As a result of the derailment, four-wheel cars were banned north of the Cabin for a couple of years. Not quite as draconian as it sounds, since there were but two - No. 513 and Stockport 5.

Below The Home closed in 1987 and in 2004 was converted into flats, known as Admiral Point. This name was also given to the stop, though not on the name-board. On 24 October 2007 Balloon 700 calls at the Abacus which replaced the Adshel.

Above During relaying in 2007/08, the Miners' Home stop was reduced to the basic H shape of tarmac. On 8 November 2009, Coronation 304 passes the Abacus shelter, which occupied most of the footpath.

Below Miners' Home stop disappeared at the end of the 2011 season, though the gates, lamp and tarmac path remain. Pantograph car 167 passes the relics on 25 May 2014.

Cavendish Road

Cavendish Road stop was introduced in 1921 - initially just for the winter months. It had a shelter of sorts from December 1925, but as it only lasted 13 years, it's unlikely to have been cast-iron like those at St Stephen's and Miners' Home.

Above Balloon 717 leaves the resin-paved Supertram stop at Cavendish Road on 7 July 2012.

Centre Cavendish Road stop around 1960, with a second-series Balloon passing the classic wooden name-board. (*Travelens*)

Bottom In 1937 the original shelter was replaced by the latest octagonal model, designed for locations with limited space. Like the other shelters between Cabin and Bispham, it was painted yellow in 1975. When photographed in June 1984, the shelter was so devoid of glass that passengers could barely see approaching trams.

Cavendish Road Shelters

Above The stop is looking more presentable in low afternoon sunlight on 14 February 2002, as Fleetwood Box car 40 passes on a driver-training run. The limited clearance between shelter and track is evident, despite the roof having been cut back. In the early 1990s the shelter had been re-glazed and - like many others - restored to green and cream as Nature intended. The angle-iron fencing has been replaced by 1970s-style.

Centre By 2009 Cavendish Road boasted a new lamp-post, a new style of name-board and a new shelter. Balloon 718 on 11 September.

Bottom The venerable cast-iron shelter had finally given way to this rather basic model.

Cavendish Road Paving

Top The Supertram stop at Cavendish Road was initially paved from platform to platform with resin panels. Flexity 009 calls on 19 July 2013.

Centre Between December 2013 and June 2014 the resin paving at all the stops along the Tramroad was replaced by a rubberised material supplied by Rosehill Rail. On 12 May 2014 the contractors, Bam Nuttall Ltd., are just starting at Cavendish Road, with Flexity 012 heading north.

Below Two days later the resin has been removed and the rubber panels are being installed. Flexity 013 arrives southbound.

11. Bispham Station

Almost time for another break in this photographic odyssey from Starr Gate to Fleetwood, as Balloon 709 reaches Bispham on 23 August 1981. There's only space here to look at the area round the tram station itself. Volume Three will cover the three-track layout just to the north.

Bispham Tram Stops

Above As at the other principal stops, there were once two southbound shelters at Bispham. Both dated from 1950 and were concrete, which was then the latest standard material. The five-bay shelter for the Promenade and Squire's Gate routes was just north of the turn-out down Red Bank Road to Bispham Depot, while the four-bay North Station shelter was south. In January 1962 twin-car 272 has loaded at the first and is passing the second.

Below The northbound stop was at the station building. It had a painted sign to augment the usual green roundel, which was on a centre pole. On the right of Coronation 321 in 1965 is the Promenade shelter. The old North Station shelter went in 1964.

Southbound Concrete Shelter

Top New OMO car 4 loads at the Promenade shelter on 29 December 1972, with two Brush cars approaching. As elsewhere, the shelter had been altered - at the request of drivers - so that the queue faced the oncoming tram. The traditional point-boy's shelter is still there. (*Peter Makinson*)

Centre Balloon 720 draws up to the southbound shelter on 23 August 1981 - a Sunday, hence the red card for route (duty) No. 18; green cards were used for the weekday service.

Below On 9 July 1985, Balloon 706 - newly named *Princess Alice* - loads at the shelter, with Brush car 626 behind. 706 re-entered service on 4 May, having been converted to open-top following a collision with 705 in 1980.

Southbound Abacus

Above The concrete shelter was removed in March 1999, and replaced in August by a single-bay Abacus. Brush car 623 loads on 9 August 2007, with Balloon 700 and Standard 147 completing an impromptu wartime re-enactment.

Below (left) The Abacus - which always looked a size too small - on 16 September 2010, with Liverpool 762 reversing.

Below (right) A new stop sign was fitted for 2011. Boat 600 loads on 3 July.

Down Red Bank Road

Top On an August evening in 1960, Pantograph car 175 stands at the top of Red Bank Road, its platform loaded with ticket boxes from Bispham Station.

Centre 175 makes its way down Red Bank Road.

Bottom The Pantograph car passes the Bispham Hotel, and turns into the depot yard.

Below Trams haven't run past the hotel for 50 years, but the sign still commemorates them.

The Northbound Stop

Top Brush car 292 or 293 (the only two still with Vs) stands at the northbound stop by the station building on 18 February 1961, while an English Electric railcoach loads at the Promenade/Squire's Gate shelter. The connection to Red Bank Road and Bispham Depot is on the right. The overhead was not connected to the southbound wire.

Centre At a deserted station on 1 January 1962, another railcoach waits by the northbound stop.

Below The station decked out with its annual illuminations in September 1971. Amidst an abundance of Balloons, No. 713 is sporting the cream bumpers which were briefly in fashion during the early 1970s.

The Northbound Stop

Above OMO cars still showed a rear destination in 1974, when car No. 1 stood at the compulsory stop on 30 June. On the right - and on each of the pictures on these two pages - is pole No. 325, which fed the overhead wire with current from Bispham sub-station. (*Peter Makinson*)

Below Careful, ladies. Brush car 634 (still wearing its Blackpool Centenary livery from 1976) meets Boat 600 on 29 May 1978. (*Alan Spencer collection*)

Dreadnought 59 arrives at Bispham behind Boat 605 on 3 June 1978, with OMO car 8 on the right. No. 59 had been restored by the Blackpool Civic Trust in 1976 to mark the centenary of the borough.

On the same day Brush car 631's guard goes into the office. By the door is a Bundy clock for recording the time of each tram. The Fleetwood Tramroad Company first installed these in 1901.

Sitting Around

Top The duty inspector takes his ease on 23 August 1981, as OMO car 6 waits its time. The Bundy clock has gone.

Bottom As part of their purchase of the Bispham Depot site in 1982, Sainsburys paid for this new sub-station. On 14 August 1983, Brush car 627 passes OMO 2.

Above A murmuration - or whatever the collective noun is - of Centenaries at Bispham on 2 June 2011. The service has been cut back from Little Bispham because No. 647 (in the distance) has failed on the southbound line. Red-liveried No. 645 has reversed, while No. 644 is waiting for orange No. 641 to cross over and tow 647 back to Rigby Road.

Below Happily the station - built in 1932 to the design of Borough Architect J.C. Robinson - survived the Supertram project. Though not a listed building, it featured as the Twentieth Century Society's *Building of the Month* in November 2012. Driver-training Flexity 001 is about to reverse onto the centre track on 19 September that year.

Flexity 004 works an Illuminations turnback on the evening of 14 September 2013.

Flexity 016 approaches the southbound stop on 7 July 2012. The platform on the left was laid so that heritage twin-car 272/T2 could unload from both cars at once.

Heritage Stops

The stops for heritage cars are just south of the station, between the staggered Supertram platforms.

Right Pantograph 167 unloads at the northbound heritage stop on 25 May 2014. 167 was on loan (for the third time) from the National Tramway Museum.

Below On 25 August 2013, Boat 227 waits at the southbound heritage stop. No. 227 received this attractive Southport-style livery in August 2013, having carried black and yellow (as No. 602) since 1989.

A Break at Bispham

Top On Saturday 20 September 2014, Flexity 011 pauses on its way to Little Bispham.

Centre Flexity 010 stands at Bispham on 19 May 2014, between two elegant buildings - J.C. Robinson's classical tram station and a Georgian-style bank, designed in 1927 by the architectural practice of Tom G. Lumb, who engineered the Tramroad itself in 1897/98.

Bottom A last look at Bispham and its tram station, on 25 May 2014. Flexity 003 takes a break on its journey along the coast to Fleetwood Ferry.

And so does this book.